The
Passive Income Hacks
50 Creative Ways to Build Wealth From Scratch ...

Henry Otasowere

The Passive Income Hacks

©Copyright 2023 Henry Otasowere, "Passive Income Hacks: 50 Creative Ways to Build Wealth from Scratch."

All rights reserved

No part of this publication may be reproduced, stored in a retrieval system, or transmitted, in any form or by any means, electronic, mechanical, photocopying, recording or otherwise, without the express written permission of the author.

Otimages Publishers

ISBN: 9798386912420

Dedication

To all the dreamers, doers, and believers who refuse to settle for a life of mediocrity. May this book serve as a guide to help you unlock your potential and build a life of financial freedom through the power of passive income. May you find inspiration, motivation, and practical advice within these pages to take action and make your dreams a reality. This book is dedicated to you, the ones who dare to dream big and work hard to make it happen.

CONTENTS

About the Author vii
Foreword viii
Acknowledgments x
Introduction 1
Part 1 3
    Chapter **1** 4
    Importance of passive income 4
Common misconceptions about passive income 10
The benefits of building passive income streams 15
Part 2 23
Passive Income Strategies That Require No Initial Investment 23
    Chapter **2** 24
    Passive Income Strategies That Require No Initial Investment 24
Affiliate marketing 28
Sponsored content and product reviews 33
Selling digital products 38
Dropshipping 42
Creating online courses 46
Part 3 50
    Chapter **4** 51
    Passive Income Strategies That Require Minimal Investment 51
Investing in dividend-paying stocks 55
Peer-to-peer lending 58
Investing in real estate crowdfunding 61

Renting out a room on Airbnb 64
Starting a blog and monetizing it 66
Part 4 71
    Chapter 5 72
    Passive Income Strategies for the Creative Entrepreneur 72
Creating a mobile app 74
Designing and selling custom merchandise 76
Monetizing your YouTube channel 78
Selling stock photography 80
Starting a podcast and monetizing it 82
Part 5 85
    Chapter 6 86
    Alternative Passive Income Strategies 86
Renting out your car 89
Renting out storage space 91
Investing in vending machines 93
Investing in billboard advertising 95
Creating an online store and dropshipping products 96
Part 6 99
    Chapter 7 100
    Navigating the Challenges of Building Passive Income 100
Overcoming the fear of failure 102
Dealing with setbacks and obstacles 104
Staying motivated and consistent 106
Focusing on the bigger picture 108
Maintaining a work-life balance 110
Building a support network 112
Part 7 115
    Chapter 8 116

v

Tips and Tricks for Maximizing Your Passive Income Potential 116
Automate your income 118
Keep track of your finances 120
Using automation tools and software 122
Diversifying your passive income streams 124
Staying up-to-date on industry trends and changes 126
Building strong relationships with customers and clients .. 128
Investing in education and self-improvement 130
Part 8 133
    Chapter 9 134
    Case Studies and Success Stories 134
Interviews with successful passive income earners 136
Real-life examples of how people have built passive income streams from scratch 137
Tips and advice from experts in the passive income field .. 140
Part 9 142
    Chapter 10 143
    Recap of the importance of passive income 143
Final thoughts and encouragement for readers to take action 144
Resources and tools for building passive income 145

About the Author

Henry Otasowere is a gifted conference speaker and pastor, imbued with divine wisdom to impart the word of God to his audience.

He operates under a powerful prophetic and healing anointing, evident in his ministry at the Voice of Healing Ministry (Ministério Voz Da Cura) in Porto, Portugal.

Henry Otasowere is a spiritual son of Prophet Joshua Iginla, founder of the Champions Royal Assembly in Abuja, Nigeria.

Having authored over 150 books, Henry Otasowere's deep love for God and people enables him to administer healing to the brokenhearted.

He is a man of great faith and full of the Holy Spirit, whose teachings and preaching have touched countless lives worldwide.

Henry Otasowere's compassionate and truthful messages reflect his genuine care for people.

Henry and his wife, prophetess Andreia Otasowere, share a strong commitment to family values and are an inspiring couple. They are passionate about living out God's plan for their lives, and their travels across the globe bring hope to hurting souls, as they radiate joy and positivity.

Foreword

We live in a time where the concept of financial freedom and independence has become increasingly important. As the world becomes more complex, so does our need for financial stability and security. The good news is that generating passive income is no longer a pipe dream or a privilege reserved for the wealthy. "Passive Income Hacks: 50 Creative Ways to Build Wealth From Scratch" is a book that will help anyone with the desire and determination to build a passive income stream.

The beauty of passive income is that it can come from a variety of sources and can be generated through a range of activities. This book covers 50 creative ways to build passive income from scratch, providing readers with a range of options to suit their interests, skills, and resources.

The author's approach is practical, informative, and comprehensive. Whether you are looking to start an online business, invest in real estate, or create a mobile app, this book has got you covered. The author's writing style is engaging, easy to understand, and will inspire you to take action.

One of the standout features of this book is the author's emphasis on building passive income streams that require no initial investment or minimal investment. This makes the strategies accessible to a wider audience and highlights the fact that building passive income is not just for the rich.

"Passive Income Hacks" is an excellent resource for anyone looking to create a more stable and secure financial future. The author's advice and tips are practical, actionable, and will help you to build a passive income stream that suits your needs and goals.

I highly recommend this book to anyone looking to create more financial freedom and independence in their lives. With "Passive Income Hacks", you will learn how to generate passive income, no matter where you are starting from.

Moreover, what I appreciate about this book is the author's ability to not only provide practical advice but also address the emotional and psychological aspects of building passive income. The author recognizes that building passive income is not just a matter of following a set of steps, but also requires discipline, perseverance, and the ability to overcome setbacks.

The book is also filled with real-life examples and success stories of people who have used these strategies to build successful passive income streams. These stories provide inspiration and motivation for readers, reminding us that with the right mindset and approach, it is possible to achieve financial freedom through passive income.

As someone who has personally experienced the benefits of passive income, I can attest to the power of these strategies. Building passive income has allowed me to pursue my passions, spend time with loved ones, and create a life that I truly enjoy. I believe that "Passive Income Hacks" will be an invaluable resource for anyone looking to do the same.

In conclusion, I highly recommend "Passive Income Hacks: 50 Creative Ways to Build Wealth From Scratch" to anyone who is serious about building a passive income stream. The author's advice is practical, actionable, and will help you to create a life of financial freedom and independence. This book is a must-read for anyone looking to take control of their financial future.

Acknowledgments

Writing a book is no small feat, and it takes a village to bring it to life. I am incredibly grateful for the support, encouragement, and inspiration that I have received throughout the process of writing "Passive Income Hacks: 50 Creative Ways to Build Wealth From Scratch."

First and foremost, I want to thank my family and friends for their unwavering support and encouragement. Your belief in me has been a constant source of motivation, and I could not have done this without you.

I also want to express my gratitude to the team at the publishing company for their guidance, expertise, and enthusiasm. Your insights and suggestions have helped to shape this book into the best possible version.

To the experts and professionals who provided me with valuable insights, advice, and feedback, I want to extend my heartfelt appreciation. Your expertise and willingness to share your knowledge have been instrumental in creating a comprehensive guide to passive income.

I would also like to thank the readers who will embark on this journey with me. It is my hope that this book will provide you with the tools, strategies, and inspiration you need to build a passive income stream that will change your life.

Finally, I want to acknowledge the power of the written word and the impact that books can have on people's lives. It is my hope that "Passive Income Hacks" will help to empower and inspire readers to take control of their financial futures and create lives of abundance and freedom.

I would also like to express my gratitude to the individuals and organizations who generously shared their success stories and insights into building passive income. Your experiences have provided valuable inspiration and motivation for readers, and I am grateful for your willingness to share your stories.

To my colleagues and mentors who have supported me throughout my career, thank you for your guidance and encouragement. Your wisdom and expertise have been invaluable in shaping my perspective on passive income and business in general.

I want to thank the countless authors, bloggers, and podcasters who have inspired and educated me on the topic of passive income. Your work has been instrumental in shaping the content of this book, and I am grateful for your contributions to the world of personal finance.

Finally, I want to acknowledge the readers who will take the time to read "Passive Income Hacks." It is my hope that this book will provide you with the knowledge, tools, and inspiration you need to build a successful passive income stream. Your interest and support mean the world to me, and I hope that you find this book to be a valuable resource on your journey to financial freedom.

Thank you all for your contributions, support, and encouragement. It is my hope that this book will help to change lives and empower people to take control of their financial futures.

Introduction

In today's fast-paced world, achieving financial freedom and independence has become a top priority for many people. Building passive income streams is an excellent way to achieve this goal, as it provides a way to earn money without having to actively trade your time for it. Passive income allows you to have the flexibility and freedom to pursue other interests, spend time with loved ones, and create a life that you truly enjoy.

However, many people are unaware of the various ways to generate passive income, and the common misconception that it requires a large initial investment can be discouraging. This is where "Passive Income Hacks: 50 Creative Ways to Build Wealth From Scratch" comes in. This book is designed to provide readers with a comprehensive guide to building passive income streams from scratch, without any initial investment.

In this book, you will discover 50 creative and unconventional ways to generate passive income, from affiliate marketing to renting out storage space. The book will also explore strategies that require minimal investment, such as investing in dividend-paying stocks or peer-to-peer lending. Additionally, the book will provide tips and tricks for maximizing your passive income potential, navigating challenges, and staying motivated.

Whether you're a seasoned entrepreneur or just starting out, "Passive Income Hacks" is an essential resource for anyone looking to build wealth and achieve financial freedom through passive income. So, let's dive in and discover the endless possibilities of generating passive income!

Passive income is not a get-rich-quick scheme, and building it takes time and effort. However, the benefits of having a steady stream of income that requires little to no effort on your part are undeniable. With passive income, you can earn money while you sleep, travel, or pursue other interests.

This book will also provide readers with alternative passive income strategies, such as investing in vending machines or billboard advertising. These options may not be as well-known as other strategies, but they offer a unique opportunity for those looking to diversify their passive income streams.

"Passive Income Hacks" will also address the challenges that come with building passive income, such as overcoming the fear of failure, dealing with setbacks, and staying motivated. The book will provide actionable tips and advice for overcoming these obstacles, as well as case studies and success stories of people who have built successful passive income streams from scratch.

Ultimately, "Passive Income Hacks" is more than just a guidebook for generating passive income. It is a tool for creating a life of freedom, flexibility, and abundance. With the information and strategies provided in this book, you will be well on your way to achieving financial independence and living life on your terms.

PART 1
Importance of passive income

CHAPTER *1*

IMPORTANCE OF PASSIVE INCOME

Passive income has become a popular topic in recent years, with more and more people realizing the importance of having a reliable source of income that does not require constant work or effort. However, many people may not be aware of the full extent of the benefits that passive income can provide, or the potential downsides of relying solely on traditional forms of income.

One important benefit of passive income is its ability to provide financial stability and security. Traditional forms of income, such as a salaried job or hourly wage, are often limited by factors such as time, availability, and market demand. In contrast, passive income streams can provide a consistent and reliable source of income that is not dependent on these factors. This can help to alleviate financial stress and provide a sense of security and peace of mind.

Another benefit of passive income is its ability to provide financial freedom and flexibility. With passive income, individuals have the ability to earn money without being tied to a specific location, schedule, or job. This can allow for greater flexibility in terms of work-life balance, travel, and pursuing hobbies and passions.

In addition, passive income can provide a way to build wealth and achieve financial goals. By reinvesting passive income streams, individuals can build a portfolio of assets that can continue to generate income over time. This can lead to greater financial independence and the ability to achieve long-term financial goals, such as early retirement or financial freedom.

However, it is important to note that not all passive income streams are created equal. Some forms of passive income may require significant upfront investment or ongoing maintenance, while others may be subject to market fluctuations or changes in demand. It is important for individuals to carefully consider their options and evaluate the potential risks and benefits of different passive income strategies.

Overall, the importance of passive income cannot be overstated. It can provide financial stability, flexibility, and the ability to achieve long-term financial goals. By understanding the potential benefits and risks of different passive income strategies, individuals can take control of their financial futures and build a life of abundance and freedom.

Many people may not be aware of the different types of passive income streams that are available to them. While some may be familiar with traditional forms of passive income, such as rental income or dividend payments from investments, there are a plethora of other options that may not be as well-known.

For example, some people may not be aware of the potential of affiliate marketing as a passive income stream. This involves promoting other people's products and earning a commission on any sales that are made through your unique referral link. Similarly, creating and selling digital products, such as e-books or online courses, can be a lucrative form of passive income that requires minimal ongoing maintenance.

Another aspect that many people may not know about is the importance of diversifying passive income streams. Relying solely on one form of passive income can be risky, as it may be subject to market fluctuations or changes in demand. By diversifying passive income streams across multiple sources, individuals can mitigate this risk and ensure a more stable and reliable source of income over time.

It is also important to note that building a passive income stream takes time and effort. While the term "passive" may suggest that no work is involved, the reality is that creating and maintaining a successful passive income stream requires dedication, patience, and a willingness to learn and adapt.

Overall, the importance of passive income cannot be understated. By understanding the potential benefits and risks of different passive income strategies and being willing to put in the work, individuals can take control of their financial futures and build a life of abundance and freedom.

Many people may not realize the potential tax benefits that can come with passive income streams. Depending on the type of passive income, individuals may be able to take advantage of various tax deductions and credits that can help to reduce their overall tax burden.

For example, owning rental property can provide numerous tax benefits, including deductions for expenses such as mortgage interest, property taxes, and repairs and maintenance. Similarly, investing in real estate through a real estate investment trust (REIT) can provide tax advantages such as the ability to defer taxes on capital gains.

In addition, many passive income streams can be structured in a way that allows for greater control over tax liability. For example, by creating a limited liability company (LLC) for rental properties or other passive income streams, individuals can take advantage of various tax benefits and deductions while also limiting their personal liability.

Finally, it is important for individuals to consider the potential impact of passive income on their overall financial picture. While passive income can provide numerous benefits, it is important to ensure that it aligns with your overall financial goals and plans. For example, individuals who are focused on paying off debt or saving for a specific financial goal may need to prioritize traditional forms of income over passive income streams in the short term.

In conclusion, passive income can be a powerful tool for achieving financial stability, flexibility, and freedom. By understanding the potential benefits, risks, and tax implications of different passive income strategies, individuals can take control of their financial futures and build a life of abundance and prosperity.

Many people may not be aware of the potential long-term benefits of passive income. While it may take time and effort to create and maintain a successful passive income stream, the rewards can be significant and lasting.

One of the primary benefits of passive income is the ability to generate income without being tied to a traditional 9-to-5 job. This can provide greater flexibility and freedom to pursue other interests, spend time with family and friends, or travel the world.

Passive income can also provide a source of income during retirement or other periods of life when traditional forms of income may be limited or unavailable. By building a diverse portfolio of passive income streams, individuals can ensure a reliable and steady stream of income over time.

In addition, passive income can provide a sense of security and stability in an unpredictable world. By diversifying income streams and creating multiple sources of passive income, individuals can protect themselves from unexpected events such as job loss, economic downturns, or other financial setbacks.

Finally, passive income can also provide a sense of accomplishment and satisfaction. Building and maintaining a successful passive income stream requires dedication, patience, and hard work. By taking control of their financial futures and building a life of abundance and prosperity, individuals can experience a sense of pride and fulfillment that comes from achieving their goals and dreams.

Overall, the potential benefits of passive income are significant and should not be overlooked. By understanding the long-term potential of passive income streams and taking the necessary steps to create and maintain them, individuals can achieve financial stability, freedom, and prosperity over time.

Another important aspect of passive income that many people may not be aware of is the power of compounding. When you invest in passive income streams, such as stocks, bonds, or real estate, your earnings can accumulate over time, generating even greater returns.

For example, if you invest in a stock that pays a 5% dividend yield, and you reinvest those dividends over a period of 20 years, your initial investment can potentially double or even triple in value. This is because the dividends you receive each year are reinvested, generating even more dividends the following year. Over time, the compounding effect can result in significant gains and a steady stream of passive income.

Additionally, many passive income strategies can provide a hedge against inflation. Inflation can erode the purchasing power of your savings and investments over time, making it difficult to maintain your standard of living. However, passive income streams such as real estate, commodities, and dividend-paying stocks have historically been effective at providing a hedge against inflation and preserving the value of your investments over time.

Finally, it's important to note that passive income can also provide a sense of purpose and fulfillment. By creating passive income streams through investments or other means, individuals can feel a sense of control over their financial future and a greater sense of security. This can lead to a greater sense of purpose and fulfillment in other areas of life, such as relationships, career, and personal growth.

In conclusion, passive income can be a powerful tool for achieving financial stability, flexibility, and freedom. By understanding the potential benefits of passive income, such as the power of compounding and a hedge against inflation, individuals can take control of their financial futures and build a life of abundance and prosperity.

Another important aspect of passive income that many people may not be aware of is the tax benefits it can provide. Certain passive income streams, such as real estate investments, can offer significant tax advantages that can help individuals reduce their tax liabilities and increase their overall net worth.

For example, rental income from real estate investments can be subject to various deductions and tax breaks, such as depreciation, property taxes, and mortgage interest. These deductions can help reduce the taxable income generated by the rental property and ultimately lower the tax liability for the investor.

Additionally, passive income streams such as dividends from stocks and mutual funds can be taxed at a lower rate than traditional income sources such as wages or salaries. This can help investors retain more of their earnings and potentially grow their investments faster over time.

Finally, passive income can also offer a form of asset protection. By investing in passive income streams, such as real estate, stocks, or bonds, individuals can protect their assets from potential creditors and legal action. This can provide greater peace of mind and a greater sense of security.

In summary, passive income can provide a range of benefits beyond just the ability to generate additional income. These benefits include tax advantages, asset protection, and a sense of control over one's financial future. By understanding these potential benefits and taking action to create and maintain passive income streams, individuals can build a solid foundation for long-term financial stability and success.

Common misconceptions about passive income

Passive income is often seen as an ideal way to create wealth and achieve financial freedom. While many people may be aware of the benefits of generating passive income, such as having more money to invest, enjoying more time and freedom, and reducing financial stress, there are also some less well-known advantages that can make passive income even more important.

One of the lesser-known benefits of passive income is that it can help individuals achieve their long-term financial goals more quickly and efficiently. This is because passive income streams often generate a continuous and reliable stream of income, which can help individuals to save and invest more money over time. This, in turn, can help them reach their financial goals, such as saving for retirement, buying a home, or paying off debt, faster than they would be able to with just their regular income.

Another important aspect of passive income that many people may not be aware of is the potential for generating income even while you sleep. Passive income streams, such as rental income from real estate, dividends from stocks, or royalties from creative works, can generate income 24/7 without requiring your constant attention or effort. This means that individuals can continue to earn money even when they're not actively working, which can provide greater financial security and freedom.

Moreover, passive income streams can provide an alternative to traditional employment or a way to supplement existing income. Many passive income streams can be started with little to no money upfront, and can be grown over time to generate significant income. This can be a particularly appealing option for those who are looking for ways to create multiple streams of income, diversify their portfolio, or achieve financial independence.

Finally, passive income can also provide a sense of satisfaction and fulfillment. By creating passive income streams through investments or other means, individuals can feel a sense of accomplishment and control over their financial future. This can lead to greater feelings of confidence, self-esteem, and overall well-being.

In conclusion, passive income can offer a range of benefits beyond just the ability to generate additional income. These benefits include helping individuals achieve their long-term financial goals more efficiently, providing a way to earn income even when not actively working, offering an alternative to traditional employment, and providing a sense of satisfaction and fulfillment. By understanding these potential advantages, individuals can take action to create and maintain passive income streams that can help them achieve their financial and personal goals.

Another important aspect of passive income that many people may not be aware of is its potential to create financial security for the future. By diversifying one's income streams with passive income, individuals can reduce their reliance on a single source of income, such as their job, and create a safety net for themselves and their families in case of unforeseen circumstances, such as a job loss or illness.

Moreover, passive income can provide a way to generate income that is not tied to the ups and downs of the economy or the job market. For example, while traditional employment may be subject to layoffs or downsizing during an economic downturn, passive income streams, such as rental income or dividends, can continue to generate income regardless of the economic climate. This can provide a sense of stability and security that is not always available through traditional employment.

In addition, passive income can offer a way to create generational wealth and financial legacy for future generations. By investing in passive income streams, individuals can create assets that can continue to generate income for their children and grandchildren, providing a long-term financial legacy that can last for many years to come.

Finally, passive income can also provide a way to give back to others and make a positive impact on the world. By using passive income streams to support charitable causes or invest in socially responsible companies, individuals can make a difference in their communities and contribute to the greater good.

In summary, passive income can offer a range of benefits that go beyond just generating additional income. These benefits include creating financial security for the future, providing stability and diversification of income, creating a long-term financial legacy, and making a positive impact on the world. By understanding these potential advantages, individuals can take steps to create and maintain passive income streams that can help them achieve their financial and personal goals while also making a difference in the world.

Another important aspect of passive income that many people may not be aware of is the ability to achieve financial freedom and independence. Passive income streams can provide a way for individuals to earn money without having to actively trade their time for it, which can allow them to work less, travel more, or pursue other interests or hobbies that they are passionate about.

Passive income can also provide a way to achieve financial goals that may seem out of reach through traditional employment. For example, passive income can provide a way to save for retirement, pay off debt, or invest in assets such as real estate or stocks that can provide long-term financial benefits.

Moreover, passive income can provide a way to create a lifestyle that aligns with one's values and priorities. By generating income through passive means, individuals can have greater control over their time and resources, which can allow them to live a more fulfilling and purposeful life.

Finally, passive income can also provide a way to build wealth and achieve financial abundance over the long term. By reinvesting passive income into additional income streams or assets, individuals can create a compounding effect that can lead to exponential growth in their wealth and net worth.

In summary, passive income can provide a path to financial freedom, independence, and abundance that may not be available through traditional employment or income sources. By understanding the potential benefits of passive income and taking steps to create and maintain passive income streams, individuals can achieve their financial goals, live a more fulfilling life, and create a lasting legacy for themselves and their families.

Another important aspect of passive income that many people may not be aware of is the potential to build a business or career around it. Many successful entrepreneurs and business owners have built their businesses around passive income streams, such as affiliate marketing, e-commerce, or online courses.

Passive income streams can provide a foundation for creating a scalable business model that can generate income on autopilot, freeing up time and resources to focus on growth and expansion. For example, an e-commerce store that generates passive income through dropshipping can be scaled up by adding new product lines or expanding into new markets, without requiring significant additional investment in time or resources.

Moreover, passive income streams can provide a way to monetize one's expertise or knowledge, creating opportunities for career growth and development. For example, an author who writes a book that generates passive income through royalties can build a career around their writing, speaking engagements, and other related activities.

Finally, passive income streams can also provide a way to create a legacy or impact beyond one's immediate career or business. By using passive income to fund charitable organizations or support social causes, individuals can make a positive impact on the world and leave a lasting legacy that goes beyond their own personal success.

In summary, passive income can provide a way to build a successful business or career that is scalable, flexible, and aligned with one's passions and expertise. By leveraging passive income streams to create a foundation for growth and expansion, individuals can achieve their professional goals, make a positive impact on the world, and create a lasting legacy that extends beyond their own personal success.

Another important aspect of passive income that many people may not be aware of is the potential to create a sense of financial security and stability. Passive income streams can provide a source of reliable and consistent income that can help to mitigate financial risks and uncertainties, such as job loss or economic downturns.

Passive income can also provide a way to diversify one's income sources and reduce reliance on traditional employment or single sources of income. By creating multiple passive income streams, individuals can spread their financial risk and increase their overall financial stability.

Moreover, passive income streams can provide a way to generate income from assets that may appreciate in value over time, such as real estate or stocks. By investing in passive income-generating assets, individuals can not only generate income but also build long-term wealth and financial security.

Finally, passive income can provide a way to reduce financial stress and anxiety, allowing individuals to focus on their personal and professional goals. By having a steady source of income that does not require constant effort or attention, individuals can have greater peace of mind and a sense of control over their financial situation.

Passive income can provide a way to achieve financial security, stability, and peace of mind by diversifying income sources, investing in income-generating assets, and reducing reliance on traditional employment or single sources of income. By understanding the potential benefits of passive income and taking steps to create and maintain passive income streams, individuals can achieve financial freedom, independence, and abundance, while also reducing financial stress and anxiety.

The benefits of building passive income streams

Building passive income streams can provide a range of benefits that many people may not be aware of. In addition to the financial benefits discussed earlier, passive income streams can also provide a range of lifestyle benefits, including increased flexibility, freedom, and creativity.

One major benefit of building passive income streams is increased flexibility. Passive income streams can provide a way to earn income on your own terms, without being tied to a specific location, employer, or schedule. This can allow you to create a more flexible and fulfilling lifestyle, with more time to pursue personal interests, spend time with family and friends, or travel the world.

Passive income streams can also provide a way to achieve greater freedom and independence. By building passive income streams, you can reduce your reliance on traditional employment or single sources of income, giving you greater control over your financial situation and greater freedom to pursue your goals and dreams.

Another benefit of building passive income streams is increased creativity and innovation. By creating passive income streams, you are essentially creating something out of nothing, whether it's a digital product, an investment portfolio, or a rental property. This requires creativity, innovation, and problem-solving skills, which can help to stimulate your mind and keep you engaged and excited about your work.

Moreover, building passive income streams can also provide a way to make a positive impact on the world. By creating passive income streams that align with your values and passions, you can make a difference in the lives of others, support important causes, and leave a positive legacy that extends beyond your own personal success.

In summary, building passive income streams can provide a range of benefits beyond financial security and stability. By creating more flexibility, freedom, creativity, and opportunities to make a positive impact, passive income streams can help to create a more fulfilling and meaningful life. By taking steps to build and maintain passive income streams, individuals can achieve financial freedom, independence, and abundance, while also creating a more fulfilling and meaningful life.

Another benefit of building passive income streams that many people may not be aware of is the potential for personal growth and development. Building passive income streams requires a range of skills and abilities, including entrepreneurship, financial literacy, marketing, and communication. By taking on the challenge of building passive income streams, individuals can develop and strengthen these skills, as well as their confidence and self-esteem.

Moreover, building passive income streams can provide a way to cultivate a growth mindset and embrace lifelong learning. In order to create and maintain successful passive income streams, individuals must be willing to continuously learn and adapt to changing market conditions, technologies, and customer needs. This can help to foster a growth mindset, which is characterized by a belief in one's ability to learn and improve over time.

Building passive income streams can also provide a way to create a sense of purpose and meaning in life. By creating income streams that align with your values and passions, you can create a sense of purpose and meaning in your work, and feel more fulfilled and satisfied with your life.

Finally, building passive income streams can provide a way to leave a lasting legacy and impact on the world. By building income streams that support important causes, contribute to the community, or provide value to others, individuals can leave a positive legacy that extends beyond their own personal success.

In summary, building passive income streams can provide a range of personal growth and development benefits, including the development of skills and abilities, the cultivation of a growth mindset, the creation of purpose and meaning, and the ability to leave a lasting legacy and impact on the world. By taking steps to build and maintain passive income streams, individuals can achieve financial freedom, independence, and abundance, while also cultivating personal growth and development.

Another benefit of building passive income streams that many people may not know is the potential for achieving financial independence and retiring early. With passive income streams, individuals can generate income without being tied to a traditional 9-5 job, which can provide more flexibility and freedom in how they spend their time. This can also allow individuals to retire early or pursue other passions and interests without worrying about financial constraints.

Passive income streams can also provide a way to diversify your income sources and protect against financial volatility. By building multiple streams of passive income, individuals can reduce their reliance on a single source of income and better weather economic downturns or unexpected financial setbacks.

Moreover, passive income streams can provide a way to create long-term wealth and financial security. Unlike active income, which is tied to the amount of time and effort put in, passive income can continue to generate income even when you are not actively working. This can allow individuals to build wealth over time and achieve financial security and abundance.

Additionally, building passive income streams can provide a way to create a legacy of wealth and prosperity for future generations. By investing in passive income streams that provide long-term returns, individuals can create a legacy of financial stability and security for their children and grandchildren.

Building passive income streams can provide a way to achieve financial independence and retire early, diversify income sources, create long-term wealth and financial security, and leave a legacy of prosperity for future generations. By understanding the potential benefits of passive income, individuals can take steps to build and maintain passive income streams that support their financial goals and aspirations.

Another benefit of building passive income streams that many people may not know is the potential to unlock greater creativity and innovation. When individuals have more financial freedom and flexibility, they can pursue new projects and ideas that they may not have had the opportunity to explore otherwise. This can lead to the discovery of new talents, interests, and passions, and ultimately lead to greater personal fulfillment and satisfaction.

Moreover, building passive income streams can provide a way to achieve greater work-life balance. When individuals have multiple sources of passive income, they can reduce the amount of time and energy spent on active income pursuits, and have more time to devote to personal pursuits, such as hobbies, travel, or spending time with family and friends.

Passive income streams can also provide a way to build a sense of community and belonging. By investing in passive income streams that support local businesses or social causes, individuals can become more connected to their community and contribute to the greater good. This can provide a sense of purpose and belonging that can be difficult to achieve through traditional active income pursuits.

Finally, building passive income streams can provide a way to overcome financial anxiety and stress. By building a reliable source of passive income, individuals can reduce the stress and anxiety associated with financial uncertainty, and enjoy greater peace of mind and mental well-being.

In summary, building passive income streams can provide a way to unlock greater creativity and innovation, achieve greater work-life balance, build a sense of community and belonging, and overcome financial anxiety and stress. By understanding the diverse benefits of passive income, individuals can take steps to build and maintain passive income streams that support their personal and financial goals, and ultimately achieve greater success and fulfillment in life.

Another benefit of building passive income streams that many people may not know is the potential to build a more resilient financial future. Passive income streams are often more stable and predictable than active income sources, as they are not tied to changes in market conditions or fluctuations in demand. This can provide greater financial stability and predictability, and allow individuals to better prepare for unexpected expenses or emergencies.

Moreover, building passive income streams can provide a way to pursue personal and professional growth without sacrificing financial stability. By building a reliable source of passive income, individuals can pursue their goals and aspirations without worrying about the financial consequences. This can provide greater peace of mind and confidence in pursuing new opportunities and taking calculated risks.

Passive income streams can also provide a way to build a more sustainable future, both financially and environmentally. By investing in passive income streams that support sustainable and socially responsible businesses or causes, individuals can contribute to a more equitable and sustainable future. This can help to build a more just and prosperous society, and provide a sense of purpose and fulfillment in making a positive impact on the world.

Finally, building passive income streams can provide a way to achieve greater financial freedom and independence. By building multiple sources of passive income, individuals can reduce their reliance on traditional employment or active income sources, and enjoy greater financial freedom and independence. This can provide greater flexibility and control over how individuals choose to spend their time and resources, and allow for greater personal and professional fulfillment.

In summary, building passive income streams can provide a way to build a more resilient financial future, pursue personal and professional growth without sacrificing financial stability, contribute to a more sustainable and socially responsible future, and achieve greater financial freedom and independence. By understanding the diverse benefits of passive income, individuals can take steps to build and maintain passive income streams that support their personal and financial goals, and ultimately achieve greater success and fulfillment in life.

Another benefit of building passive income streams that many people may not know is the potential to create generational wealth. Unlike active income, which is typically tied to an individual's skills or abilities, passive income can continue to generate income for future generations with little to no effort required. This can provide a way to create a lasting legacy and ensure financial security for future generations.

Furthermore, building passive income streams can provide a way to diversify one's income and reduce financial risk. Relying solely on one source of income, such as a job, can leave individuals vulnerable to economic downturns, job loss, or other unexpected events. By building multiple sources of passive income, individuals can spread their financial risk and ensure a more stable and secure financial future.

In addition, building passive income streams can provide a way to accelerate wealth-building and achieve financial goals faster. By reinvesting passive income back into new income streams or other investments, individuals can compound their wealth over time and accelerate their path to financial freedom.

Building passive income streams can provide a way to achieve greater work-life balance and reduce stress. By reducing reliance on traditional employment or active income sources, individuals can enjoy more time for personal pursuits, family, and leisure activities. This can lead to a greater sense of fulfillment and satisfaction in life, and ultimately contribute to better physical and mental health.

Building passive income streams can provide numerous benefits, including the potential to create generational wealth, diversify income and reduce financial risk, accelerate wealth-building and achieve financial goals faster, and achieve greater work-life balance and reduce stress. By understanding the diverse benefits of passive income, individuals can take steps to build and maintain passive income streams that support their personal and financial goals, and ultimately achieve greater success and fulfillment in life.

Another benefit of building passive income streams that many people may not be aware of is the potential tax benefits. Some types of passive income, such as rental income from real estate, may be subject to more favorable tax treatment compared to active income. For example, rental income can often be offset by deductions such as mortgage interest, property taxes, and depreciation, which can significantly reduce the amount of taxable income.

In addition, some passive income streams, such as investments in tax-advantaged accounts like IRAs or 401(k)s, may offer additional tax benefits such as tax-deferred or tax-free growth.

Another benefit of passive income is the potential to leverage other people's time and resources to generate income. For example, investing in a real estate syndicate or crowdfunding platform can allow individuals to pool their resources with others to invest in larger, higher-yield real estate projects that would be difficult or impossible to achieve on their own. This can provide a way to generate passive income without having to personally manage the investment.

Building passive income streams can provide a way to pursue personal interests and passions while still generating income. For example, individuals who love to write can earn passive income through self-publishing books or creating online courses. Those with a passion for photography can generate passive income through licensing their images or selling prints online. By pursuing their passions while still earning income, individuals can achieve greater fulfillment and satisfaction in their lives.

Building passive income streams can provide numerous benefits beyond just the financial rewards. From tax benefits to leveraging the resources of others to pursuing personal passions, passive income can offer a way to achieve greater freedom, flexibility, and fulfillment in life. By understanding the diverse benefits of passive income and taking steps to build and maintain passive income streams, individuals can achieve greater success and fulfillment in all aspects of their lives.

PART 2

Passive Income Strategies That Require No Initial Investment

CHAPTER *2*

PASSIVE INCOME STRATEGIES THAT REQUIRE NO INITIAL INVESTMENT

Passive income is often associated with the need for a significant amount of capital upfront in order to generate a return. However, there are also passive income strategies that require no initial investment, which can be a great option for those who are just starting out or have limited resources.

One such strategy is affiliate marketing. Affiliate marketing involves promoting other people's products and services through a unique link, and earning a commission on any sales that result from that link. This can be done through a blog, social media, or other online platforms, and requires no upfront investment other than time and effort.

Another passive income strategy that requires no initial investment is creating digital products such as e-books, online courses, or printables. These products can be sold through platforms such as Etsy, Amazon, or your own website, and can generate ongoing income without requiring ongoing effort.

Investing in dividend-paying stocks is another way to generate passive income without any initial investment. By investing in companies that pay out regular dividends to shareholders, individuals can earn a steady stream of income without having to constantly monitor or manage their investments.

Another strategy is creating and monetizing a YouTube channel. While there may be some initial costs associated with purchasing equipment such as a camera or microphone, it is possible to start a YouTube channel with just a smartphone and basic editing software. By creating valuable content and growing a following, individuals can earn passive income through advertising revenue and sponsorships.

Finally, individuals can also generate passive income through renting out unused space in their home, such as a spare bedroom or parking space. Platforms such as Airbnb and ParkWhiz make it easy to rent out space to others and earn income without any initial investment.

In conclusion, while many passive income strategies do require upfront capital, there are also several options that require no initial investment. By exploring these strategies and finding the ones that align with their skills and interests, individuals can generate ongoing income without having to invest a significant amount of money upfront.

One more passive income strategy that requires no initial investment is creating and monetizing a podcast. Podcasting is a popular medium that allows individuals to create audio content on a particular topic, and build a following of loyal listeners. By monetizing their podcast through sponsorships, affiliate marketing, or merchandise sales, individuals can generate a steady stream of passive income.

Another strategy is creating and selling stock photos or videos. If an individual has a talent for photography or videography, they can create a portfolio of high-quality content and sell it on platforms such as Shutterstock or iStock. Once the content is uploaded, it can generate ongoing income without any further effort.

Another passive income strategy that requires no initial investment is peer-to-peer lending. Platforms such as LendingClub or Prosper allow individuals to lend money to others and earn interest on their investment. While there is some risk involved in this strategy, it can be a way to generate ongoing income without requiring any upfront capital.

Additionally, individuals can also generate passive income by renting out their vehicle through platforms such as Turo or Getaround. By allowing others to rent their car for a fee, individuals can earn ongoing income without any initial investment other than the cost of their vehicle.

Finally, individuals can also earn passive income by participating in cashback rewards programs. Platforms such as Rakuten or Honey offer cashback rewards for online purchases made through their platform. By simply signing up and making purchases through these platforms, individuals can earn ongoing passive income in the form of cashback rewards.

In summary, while there are many passive income strategies that require upfront capital, there are also several options that require no initial investment. By exploring these strategies and finding the ones that align with their skills and interests, individuals can generate ongoing income without having to invest a significant amount of money upfront.

Another passive income strategy that requires no initial investment is affiliate marketing. Affiliate marketing involves promoting other people's products or services and earning a commission for each sale made through your unique affiliate link. This can be done through various mediums such as social media, blogs, or YouTube channels.

Another option is creating and monetizing a YouTube channel. By creating engaging video content and building a following, individuals can generate passive income through advertising revenue, sponsorships, and merchandise sales.

Another passive income strategy is participating in online surveys and focus groups. While this may not generate a significant amount of income, it can be a way to earn some extra cash without requiring any initial investment.

Finally, individuals can also earn passive income by writing and publishing an e-book on platforms such as Amazon Kindle Direct Publishing. By creating an e-book on a particular topic and marketing it effectively, individuals can generate ongoing income without any upfront investment.

In summary, there are several passive income strategies that require no initial investment, including affiliate marketing, creating a YouTube channel, participating in online surveys and focus groups, and publishing an e-book. By exploring these options and finding the ones that align with their skills and interests, individuals can generate ongoing income without having to invest any money upfront.

One lesser-known strategy for generating passive income without an initial investment is by creating and selling digital products. This can include things like printables, templates, stock photos, or digital art. By creating these products and selling them through online marketplaces like Etsy, Creative Market, or Society6, individuals can earn ongoing income without any upfront costs.

Another strategy is to start a blog or website and monetize it through display ads, sponsored content, or affiliate marketing. While there may be some initial costs associated with creating a website or blog, there are many free or low-cost options available, such as WordPress or Blogger.

Another way to earn passive income without an initial investment is through peer-to-peer lending platforms, such as Lending Club or Prosper. By lending money to other individuals or businesses, individuals can earn ongoing interest income without having to invest any money upfront.

Finally, individuals can also generate passive income by investing in dividend-paying stocks or exchange-traded funds (ETFs). These investments pay out regular dividends to shareholders, providing an ongoing source of income without requiring any initial investment beyond the cost of the stock or ETF.

In summary, there are several strategies for generating passive income without an initial investment, including creating and selling digital products, monetizing a blog or website, peer-to-peer lending, and investing in dividend-paying stocks or ETFs. By exploring these options and finding the ones that align with their skills and interests, individuals can generate ongoing income without having to invest any money upfront.

Affiliate marketing

Affiliate marketing is a popular passive income strategy that involves promoting other people's products or services and earning a commission for each sale made through a unique affiliate link. While many people are familiar with the concept of affiliate marketing, there are some lesser-known aspects of this strategy that could be beneficial for those looking to make a passive income.

One important aspect of affiliate marketing that many people do not know about is the importance of choosing the right niche. By selecting a niche that aligns with their interests and expertise, affiliates can create content that resonates with their target audience and drives sales more effectively. It's also important to choose products or services that are high-quality and have a good reputation, as this can impact the affiliate's credibility and ultimately their earnings.

Another key element of affiliate marketing is building an audience and establishing trust with them. By creating valuable content, engaging with their audience, and providing honest and transparent reviews of products, affiliates can build a loyal following that is more likely to make a purchase through their affiliate links. This can take time and effort, but it's an essential step in creating a successful affiliate marketing strategy.

Many people also overlook the importance of tracking and analyzing their affiliate marketing efforts. By using tools such as Google Analytics or affiliate tracking software, affiliates can monitor their sales, track their earnings, and analyze their marketing efforts to optimize their strategy for better results. This data can help affiliates make informed decisions about which products to promote, which marketing channels to focus on, and how to improve their overall strategy.

Finally, it's worth noting that affiliate marketing is not a get-rich-quick scheme and requires consistent effort and dedication to generate a significant passive income. Successful affiliates typically have a strong work ethic, are persistent in their efforts, and are constantly looking for ways to improve their strategy and grow their audience.

In conclusion, affiliate marketing can be a lucrative and rewarding passive income strategy, but it requires careful planning, strategic thinking, and ongoing effort. By choosing the right niche, building an audience, analyzing their efforts, and being persistent in their approach, affiliates can create a sustainable source of passive income through affiliate marketing.

Another important aspect of affiliate marketing that many people overlook is the potential for recurring commissions. Recurring commissions allow affiliates to earn a commission on a recurring basis for as long as the customer continues to use the product or service. This can be a valuable source of passive income, as it allows affiliates to earn money on a continuous basis without having to continually generate new sales.

Furthermore, it's important for affiliates to disclose their affiliate relationship and be transparent with their audience. This means clearly disclosing that they will earn a commission if someone makes a purchase through their affiliate link. By being upfront and honest with their audience, affiliates can build trust and credibility, which can ultimately lead to more sales and a stronger reputation.

Affiliate marketing can also be a versatile strategy, as it can be combined with other passive income streams to create a diversified portfolio. For example, an affiliate marketer may also have a blog or a YouTube channel where they generate ad revenue or sell their own products. By combining different passive income streams, affiliates can create multiple sources of income that can help them achieve financial independence and stability.

Finally, while affiliate marketing can be a great source of passive income, it's important to be mindful of potential scams or unethical practices. Some affiliate programs may be pyramid schemes or require affiliates to engage in spammy or deceptive marketing tactics. It's important for affiliates to thoroughly research any program they are considering and only work with reputable companies that align with their values and ethics.

In summary, affiliate marketing is a popular and effective passive income strategy that offers many benefits, including the potential for recurring commissions and the ability to combine with other income streams. However, it requires careful planning, transparency, and a commitment to ethical practices. By following best practices and staying vigilant, affiliates can build a successful and sustainable passive income stream through affiliate marketing.

Another important aspect of affiliate marketing that many people may not be aware of is the variety of affiliate programs available. Affiliate programs exist in a wide range of industries and niches, from fashion and beauty to technology and finance. This means that affiliate marketers can choose programs that align with their interests and expertise, which can make promoting products and services more enjoyable and effective.

In addition, many affiliate programs offer a variety of marketing materials, such as banners, text links, and product images, that affiliates can use on their websites or social media channels. These materials can help affiliates promote products more effectively and attract more sales.

Another advantage of affiliate marketing is that it can be relatively easy to get started. Many affiliate programs are free to join, and some require only a simple application process. Once accepted, affiliates can start promoting products and earning commissions right away, without needing to create their own products or services.

However, while affiliate marketing can be an effective way to generate passive income, it's important to note that success requires effort and commitment. Affiliates need to actively promote products and build relationships with their audience in order to maximize their earning potential. This means creating high-quality content, engaging with followers on social media, and continually testing and refining their marketing strategies.

In summary, affiliate marketing is a versatile and accessible passive income strategy that offers many benefits, including a variety of programs to choose from, a range of marketing materials, and relatively low startup costs. However, it requires effort, commitment, and a willingness to continually improve and adapt marketing strategies.

Another important aspect of affiliate marketing that many people may not be aware of is the potential for recurring commissions. Unlike other passive income strategies where earnings may be one-time or sporadic, affiliate marketing can provide ongoing commissions for as long as a customer continues to use a product or service.

For example, many software companies offer affiliate programs that pay commissions on a recurring basis for as long as the customer continues to use the software. This means that affiliates can earn passive income from a single referral over a long period of time, providing a reliable stream of income.

Another advantage of affiliate marketing is the potential for high commissions. Depending on the program and product, affiliates can earn commissions ranging from a few percent to upwards of 50% or more. This means that even a few successful referrals can generate significant income.

It's also worth noting that affiliate marketing can be combined with other passive income strategies to further increase earnings. For example, affiliates can use email marketing to promote products to their audience and generate passive income through automated email sequences.

However, it's important to note that while affiliate marketing can be a lucrative passive income strategy, it's not a get-rich-quick scheme. Success requires a solid understanding of the industry, a commitment to building relationships with audiences, and the ability to create high-quality content that resonates with potential customers.

In summary, affiliate marketing offers many benefits as a passive income strategy, including the potential for recurring and high commissions, as well as the ability to combine with other strategies. However, it requires effort, commitment, and a willingness to continually improve and adapt marketing strategies in order to be successful.

Another key advantage of affiliate marketing is the low barrier to entry. Unlike many other passive income strategies that may require significant upfront investment, affiliate marketing can be started with little to no cost. Affiliate programs are typically free to join, and many provide marketing materials and support to help affiliates get started.

This low barrier to entry also makes affiliate marketing a great option for those who may not have their own products or services to sell. Instead, affiliates can promote products and services that they believe in and earn commissions for successful referrals. This can be particularly beneficial for those who are just starting out in their entrepreneurial journey and may not have the resources to develop their own products or services.

Additionally, affiliate marketing allows for a high degree of flexibility and scalability. Affiliates can choose which products and services to promote, and can adjust their strategies and campaigns to optimize their earnings. As they become more experienced and successful, affiliates can also expand their reach by promoting products across different platforms and audiences.

It's also worth noting that affiliate marketing can be a passive income strategy that fits a variety of niches and industries. From fashion and beauty to finance and technology, there are affiliate programs available for a wide range of products and services. This means that regardless of your interests or expertise, there may be opportunities for you to earn passive income through affiliate marketing.

In conclusion, affiliate marketing offers many benefits as a low-cost and flexible passive income strategy. It can be started with little to no investment, and allows for scalability and the ability to promote products across different niches and industries. However, success requires effort, commitment, and a willingness to continually learn and adapt to changes in the industry.

Sponsored content and product reviews

Sponsored content and product reviews are another effective way to generate passive income. Many businesses are willing to pay content creators to promote their products or services through sponsored content, which can take the form of blog posts, videos, social media posts, or other types of content.

One advantage of sponsored content is that it allows content creators to earn money while providing valuable information and recommendations to their audience. By partnering with brands and promoting products that align with their values and niche, content creators can maintain authenticity and build trust with their followers.

In addition to sponsored content, product reviews can also be a lucrative way to generate passive income. Many businesses will send free products to content creators in exchange for an honest review or endorsement. Content creators can then monetize their reviews by including affiliate links or sponsored content alongside their review.

It's important to note that sponsored content and product reviews should always be transparent and honest. Content creators should disclose any partnerships or compensation received, and should only promote products that they truly believe in and have tested themselves. By maintaining transparency and integrity, content creators can build a loyal audience and establish themselves as a trusted source of information and recommendations.

Furthermore, sponsored content and product reviews can be a great opportunity for content creators to expand their reach and grow their audience. By partnering with brands and collaborating with other content creators, they can tap into new audiences and increase their exposure.

In conclusion, sponsored content and product reviews are an effective way to generate passive income for content creators. They provide a way to monetize valuable content and recommendations while maintaining authenticity and building trust with an audience. However, it's important to always be transparent and honest, and to only promote products that align with your values and niche.

Another benefit of sponsored content and product reviews is that they can lead to long-term partnerships and collaborations with brands. As content creators build a reputation for providing valuable recommendations and authentic content, brands may reach out to them directly to collaborate on future projects or sponsorships.

In addition, sponsored content and product reviews can also provide valuable insights and feedback to businesses. By working with content creators, businesses can gain feedback on their products or services and learn more about their target audience. This information can be used to improve their offerings and better serve their customers.

One potential challenge of sponsored content and product reviews is maintaining objectivity and authenticity. Content creators may feel pressure to provide positive reviews in order to maintain their partnerships with brands, even if they don't truly believe in the product. To avoid this, it's important to only partner with brands and promote products that align with your values and niche.

Furthermore, sponsored content and product reviews may not be suitable for all content creators. Those who prioritize editorial independence or have a smaller audience may not be able to command the same level of compensation as larger content creators with established partnerships and sponsorships.

Overall, sponsored content and product reviews are a viable way to generate passive income and provide valuable content to an audience. As with any monetization strategy, it's important to approach them with transparency and authenticity, and to only promote products and services that align with your values and niche.

Another consideration when it comes to sponsored content and product reviews is disclosure. It's important for content creators to be transparent about any sponsored content or product reviews they share with their audience. This can be done by including a disclaimer at the beginning or end of the content indicating that it is sponsored or that the product was provided for review purposes.

Failure to disclose sponsored content or product reviews can result in a loss of trust and credibility with an audience, which can ultimately harm a content creator's brand and future earning potential.

In addition, content creators should also consider the potential legal implications of sponsored content and product reviews. In some jurisdictions, there may be laws and regulations governing the disclosure of sponsored content and the accuracy of product reviews. It's important to research and comply with any relevant laws and regulations in your area.

Finally, when it comes to sponsored content and product reviews, it's important to maintain a balance between sponsored and non-sponsored content. While sponsored content can be a lucrative source of passive income, it's important to ensure that it does not overshadow the rest of your content and diminish the overall value provided to your audience.

Overall, sponsored content and product reviews can be a valuable source of passive income for content creators. However, it's important to approach them with transparency, authenticity, and compliance with any relevant laws and regulations. With the right approach, content creators can monetize their content while maintaining their audience's trust and providing valuable insights to businesses.

Another aspect of sponsored content and product reviews that many people may not be aware of is the potential for long-term partnerships and collaborations. When a content creator successfully partners with a brand for a sponsored campaign or product review, it can lead to future opportunities for collaboration and continued passive income.

For example, a content creator who creates sponsored content for a beauty brand may be offered the opportunity to collaborate on future product launches or events, which can lead to ongoing passive income. Similarly, a content creator who successfully reviews a technology product may be offered the opportunity to review future products from the same company.

These long-term partnerships and collaborations can be particularly lucrative for content creators, as they provide a reliable and consistent source of passive income over time. They can also help to build a content creator's brand and reputation within a particular niche, which can lead to even more opportunities for passive income in the future.

However, it's important for content creators to approach these partnerships and collaborations with authenticity and integrity. They should only partner with brands and products that they genuinely believe in and that align with their audience's interests and values. This will help to maintain their credibility and trust with their audience, which is essential for long-term success in the world of sponsored content and product reviews.

Another thing that people may not know about sponsored content and product reviews is that there are specific rules and regulations that content creators must follow. In many countries, including the United States, the Federal Trade Commission (FTC) requires that content creators disclose any sponsored content or product reviews to their audience.

This means that content creators must clearly indicate when they have been paid or compensated to create a piece of content or review a product. This can be done through a disclaimer at the beginning or end of the content, or through other methods such as hashtags or symbols.

Failing to disclose sponsored content or product reviews can result in legal consequences and damage to a content creator's reputation.

It's important for content creators to understand and follow these rules in order to maintain their credibility and trust with their audience.

In addition to disclosure requirements, content creators should also consider the ethical implications of sponsored content and product reviews. They should only promote products or brands that they genuinely believe in and that align with their values and the interests of their audience. Promoting products solely for financial gain can damage their reputation and ultimately harm their long-term success as a content creator.

By approaching sponsored content and product reviews with authenticity, integrity, and transparency, content creators can build trust with their audience and create valuable, long-term partnerships that can provide a reliable source of passive income.

Selling digital products

Selling digital products is a popular way to generate passive income online. Digital products can include anything that can be delivered electronically, such as eBooks, courses, software, templates, graphics, music, and more.

One thing that many people may not know about selling digital products is that there are many different platforms and marketplaces available for content creators to sell their products. These can include websites such as Gumroad, Payhip, and Selz, as well as larger marketplaces such as Amazon and Etsy.

Another important consideration when selling digital products is pricing. Many content creators may assume that they need to price their products low in order to attract buyers, but this is not always the case. Pricing strategies will vary depending on the product, audience, and competition, and it's important to do research and testing to find the optimal price point.

Additionally, creating high-quality digital products that provide real value to customers is crucial. Content creators should focus on creating products that solve a specific problem or provide a solution to a particular need. They should also consider offering bonuses or extras to add value to their product and incentivize customers to make a purchase.

Finally, promoting and marketing digital products is a key factor in generating sales and passive income. Content creators should leverage their social media and email lists to promote their products and consider running paid advertising campaigns to reach a wider audience.

By understanding the various platforms and marketplaces available, pricing strategies, creating high-quality products, and promoting effectively, content creators can successfully sell digital products and generate a reliable source of passive income.

You don't need to be a professional designer or developer: While some digital products may require specialized skills, such as coding for software, many can be created with basic software or tools. For example, you can create and sell ebooks, printables, or stock photos using free or affordable software like Canva or Adobe Creative Suite.

The market for digital products is growing: With the rise of e-learning and remote work, there is an increasing demand for digital products such as online courses, e-books, and software. According to a report by ResearchAndMarkets.com, the global digital content market is expected to reach $367 billion by 2026.

You can sell digital products on various platforms: There are numerous platforms that allow you to sell digital products, including Etsy, Gumroad, Shopify, and Teachable. Each platform has its own fees and features, so it's important to research and choose the one that best fits your needs.

There are different types of digital products to sell: You can sell various types of digital products, including e-books, templates, printables, music, video tutorials, and software. The key is to choose a product that aligns with your skills and interests, and that also solves a problem or meets a need for your target audience.

Marketing is key: While creating high-quality digital products is important, marketing is equally essential for generating sales. You can use various marketing strategies, such as social media marketing, email marketing, and influencer marketing, to reach your target audience and promote your products.

Overall, selling digital products can be a lucrative and rewarding way to generate passive income. With the right skills, tools, and marketing strategies, anyone can create and sell digital products online.

Digital products can have a high profit margin: Unlike physical products, digital products do not require any manufacturing, shipping, or storage costs, which can result in a high profit margin. Once the initial time investment is made to create the product, the potential for recurring revenue is significant.

Digital products can be easily scaled: As digital products can be replicated infinitely, they can be easily scaled up to reach a larger audience without incurring additional costs. This means that the potential for earning passive income increases as the product gains popularity.

Digital products can offer flexibility: Depending on the type of digital product being sold, it can be possible to sell it through various channels such as online marketplaces, personal websites, social media, and more. This offers a level of flexibility for the seller to experiment with different sales channels and find what works best for them.

Different types of digital products can be sold: There are various types of digital products that can be sold as passive income, including ebooks, online courses, software, printables, and more. This means that there are many opportunities for creators to find a niche that they are passionate about and create a product that appeals to their target audience.

It's important to choose the right pricing strategy: Pricing can have a significant impact on the success of selling digital products. Some common pricing strategies include one-time fees, subscription-based models, or tiered pricing based on the product features. It's essential to understand the target audience and the market demand to choose the best pricing strategy for the product.

Marketing is key: While creating a high-quality digital product is important, marketing the product is equally important. This involves identifying the target audience, creating a marketing plan, and leveraging various marketing channels to reach the audience effectively. By building a strong marketing strategy, it's possible to generate ongoing passive income from digital products.

Here are some more things that many people may not know about selling digital products for passive income:

The types of digital products you can sell: Digital products come in various forms, and you don't have to be an artist, writer, or developer to create them. Some examples of digital products you can sell include e-books, online courses, templates, printables, stock photos, graphics, music, and software.

The tools and platforms to use: You can create and sell digital products using various tools and platforms, including WordPress plugins like Easy Digital Downloads, e-commerce platforms like Gumroad and Shopify, and course platforms like Teachable and Thinkific. Each platform has its own features and pricing, so it's essential to research which one suits your needs and budget.

The importance of packaging and pricing: Packaging your digital products in an appealing way can make a big difference in sales. For example, bundling multiple products together can increase their perceived value and lead to more sales. Additionally, pricing your products correctly is critical. Pricing too high can lead to fewer sales, while pricing too low can lower the perceived value of your product.

The benefits of creating a sales funnel: A sales funnel is a marketing strategy that involves guiding a potential customer through a series of steps to convert them into a paying customer. By creating a sales funnel for your digital products, you can automate the sales process and increase the likelihood of making a sale.

The importance of marketing and promotion: Selling digital products requires marketing and promotion to get your products in front of potential customers. Some effective ways to market digital products include email marketing, social media advertising, influencer marketing, and content marketing.

Overall, selling digital products can be an excellent way to generate passive income, but it requires some upfront work to create and market your products effectively.

Dropshipping

Dropshipping is a type of retail fulfillment method where an online store doesn't keep the products it sells in stock. Instead, when a customer places an order, the store purchases the product from a third-party supplier who then ships it directly to the customer.

One thing that many people do not know about dropshipping is that it can be a highly profitable passive income stream if done correctly. However, it's important to note that dropshipping does come with its own set of challenges.

One lesser-known benefit of dropshipping is that it allows entrepreneurs to test out new product ideas without having to invest in inventory upfront. This means that you can quickly and easily launch a new product line and gauge its success without taking on the financial risk of purchasing large quantities of inventory.

Another thing that many people do not know about dropshipping is that it's possible to source products directly from manufacturers, which can significantly reduce the cost of goods sold. This can allow for a higher profit margin on each sale.

However, there are also some downsides to dropshipping. One of the biggest challenges is that the quality of the products can be difficult to control, as you're relying on a third-party supplier to handle the fulfillment process. Additionally, shipping times can be longer, which may lead to customer complaints and negative reviews.

Overall, dropshipping can be an effective way to build a passive income stream if approached with a solid strategy and a willingness to navigate its unique challenges.

Importance of Finding the Right Suppliers: One of the most critical aspects of successful dropshipping is finding the right suppliers. Many people make the mistake of selecting suppliers solely based on price, but quality, reliability, and shipping times are also essential factors to consider. It's also important to choose suppliers who specialize in the products you plan to sell to ensure you are offering high-quality items to your customers.

Building Relationships with Suppliers: Building strong relationships with your suppliers is essential for long-term success in dropshipping. By communicating effectively, being transparent about your business goals, and providing timely payments, you can establish trust and reliability with your suppliers. This can lead to more favorable terms, such as better pricing, faster shipping, and even exclusive products.

Navigating Shipping and Customs: Shipping and customs can be a challenge in dropshipping, especially when working with international suppliers. It's important to research and understand the shipping options available and factor in shipping times when estimating delivery dates to your customers. You'll also need to navigate customs regulations and fees, which can be time-consuming and costly if not properly planned for.

Balancing Profit Margins and Competitive Pricing: Dropshipping can be a highly competitive market, so it's essential to find a balance between profit margins and competitive pricing. While you don't want to price your products too high, you also don't want to undercut your competition to the point where you aren't making a profit. Finding the right balance requires research and testing to determine the optimal pricing strategy for your business.

Dealing with Returns and Customer Service: As the middleman between customers and suppliers, dropshippers are responsible for handling returns and customer service inquiries. It's important to have clear policies in place for returns and to be responsive and helpful when dealing with customer inquiries. By providing excellent customer service, you can build trust and loyalty with your customers, which can lead to repeat business and positive reviews.

Managing Cash Flow: Dropshipping can be a cash-intensive business, especially when working with suppliers who require upfront payment for products. To manage cash flow effectively, it's important to have a clear understanding of your expenses and revenue and to have a plan in place for managing inventory and paying suppliers. Proper cash flow management can help ensure the long-term viability and success of your dropshipping business.

Understanding Legal and Tax Implications: As with any business, dropshipping has legal and tax implications that must be considered. It's important to understand the legal requirements for selling products in your area, including any permits or licenses required. You'll also need to navigate tax regulations and ensure you are collecting and remitting sales tax correctly. Failing to comply with legal and tax requirements can result in fines and legal issues that can be detrimental to your business.

Dropshipping is a business model where the retailer doesn't hold inventory of the products they sell, instead, they partner with a supplier who ships the products directly to the customers. Here are some additional things many people might not know about dropshipping:

Niche selection is crucial: The success of a dropshipping business heavily relies on the niche selection. The right niche can bring a steady stream of customers, while the wrong one can be a complete disaster. It's important to research and find a niche with high demand and low competition.

Finding reliable suppliers can be a challenge: While dropshipping eliminates the need for inventory management, it comes with its own set of challenges. One of the biggest challenges is finding reliable suppliers who can provide quality products at reasonable prices. It's important to thoroughly research and vet potential suppliers before partnering with them.

Branding is key: With dropshipping, the retailer doesn't physically handle the products, which can make it harder to differentiate themselves from the competition. Branding becomes essential to creating a unique identity and building customer loyalty.

Customer service is critical: With dropshipping, the supplier is responsible for shipping and handling, but the retailer is still responsible for customer service. Providing exceptional customer service is critical to building a good reputation and ensuring repeat business.

Marketing and advertising are essential: As with any business, marketing and advertising are critical to building brand awareness and attracting customers. Dropshippers must develop a solid marketing strategy to reach potential customers and stand out in a crowded market.

Creating online courses

Creating and selling online courses is a popular passive income strategy that has gained significant popularity in recent years. However, there are some lesser-known aspects of this strategy that many people may not be aware of. Here are some additional details:

Choose a profitable niche: When creating an online course, it's essential to choose a profitable niche that has a large audience and a willingness to pay for high-quality content. Conducting market research can help you identify a niche that is in demand and has the potential for generating significant revenue.

Focus on solving specific problems: Successful online courses often focus on solving specific problems that learners face. By providing a practical solution to a specific problem, you can create a loyal following of learners who will continue to seek your expertise in the future.

Leverage various mediums: Online courses don't have to be limited to video lectures. You can incorporate various mediums such as text-based content, interactive quizzes, and hands-on activities to make your course more engaging and dynamic.

Provide ongoing support: Once you create an online course, providing ongoing support to learners can help establish you as an authority figure and build a sense of community. This can include hosting live Q&A sessions, creating online forums, and providing personalized feedback.

Monetize your course: There are various ways to monetize your online course, such as offering premium content or charging for certifications. Additionally, you can leverage affiliate marketing or offer your course on other platforms to reach a wider audience.

Keep updating your content: As technology and industries continue to evolve, it's essential to keep your course content updated to remain relevant and provide value to learners. This can also help keep your course ranking high in search results and increase its visibility.

Overall, creating online courses is a lucrative way to generate passive income if you're willing to put in the effort to create high-quality content, engage with learners, and market your course effectively.

Finding a profitable niche: One key to success with online courses is to find a profitable niche that you can target. This may require some research to identify a topic that is in demand and doesn't have too much competition. You can use tools like Google Trends, social media, and forums to see what topics people are talking about and what problems they need help with.

Designing effective course content: Once you've identified a niche, you'll need to create course content that is engaging, informative, and effective at teaching your students. This can involve creating videos, writing articles, developing interactive quizzes, and more. It's important to make sure your course content is well-organized and easy to follow, and that you provide plenty of examples and practical exercises to help your students apply what they're learning.

Choosing a platform: There are many platforms available for creating and selling online courses, including Udemy, Teachable, and Thinkific. Each platform has its own features and pricing structure, so you'll need to do some research to find the one that best fits your needs. You may also want to consider hosting your course on your own website using a plugin like LearnDash or LifterLMS.

Promoting your course: Once your course is ready to go, you'll need to promote it to your target audience. This can involve creating a landing page, running ads on social media, and reaching out to influencers in your niche to see if they will promote your course to their followers. You may also want to consider offering a free preview or trial of your course to encourage people to sign up.

Continuing to improve your course: Finally, it's important to continue to refine and improve your course over time. This can involve updating your content as new information becomes available, responding to feedback from students, and incorporating new features and tools to enhance the learning experience. By constantly striving to make your course better, you can attract more students and increase your passive income over time.

Niche expertise: Online courses can be created for virtually any topic, but the most successful courses are typically those that provide in-depth knowledge on a particular subject or skill. Consider your own areas of expertise or passion, and identify what topics you could teach with authority.

Learning platforms: There are a variety of learning platforms available to host your course, including Udemy, Skillshare, and Teachable. Each platform has its own requirements and fee structures, so it's important to research and compare before choosing a platform.

Course structure: A successful online course is structured in a way that is engaging and easy to follow. Consider breaking your course down into modules, including quizzes or assessments to help learners track their progress.

Marketing: Once you've created your course, you'll need to market it to potential learners. This can include leveraging social media, creating promotional videos, or partnering with other influencers in your niche.

Continued growth: To continue generating passive income from your online course, it's important to keep it up-to-date and relevant. Consider adding new content or updating existing content as the industry or subject matter evolves.

By keeping these factors in mind, you can create an online course that not only generates passive income, but also helps learners develop new skills and knowledge.

Online courses are a great way to earn passive income because they can be created once and sold repeatedly. However, many people do not realize the potential of creating online courses in niche areas. For example, there is a growing demand for online courses on niche topics such as gardening, cooking, and yoga. By creating an online course on a specific niche topic, you can differentiate yourself from the competition and attract a dedicated audience.

Another thing that many people do not know is that you don't need to be an expert to create an online course. Of course, having expertise in a particular field is helpful, but it's not a requirement. You can also create a course on a topic that you're interested in and research it thoroughly before creating the course. This can be a great way to learn more about a topic while also earning passive income.

Another thing to keep in mind is that creating an online course requires more than just creating content. You also need to have a marketing plan in place to promote your course and attract students. This can include strategies such as creating a website, building an email list, and leveraging social media platforms to reach your target audience.

Lastly, it's important to continually update and improve your course to ensure that it remains relevant and valuable to your students. This can involve incorporating student feedback, updating content to reflect changes in your industry or niche, and keeping up with technological advancements to ensure that your course remains engaging and user-friendly. By continually improving your course, you can attract new students and earn a steady stream of passive income.

PART 3
Passive Income Strategies That Require Minimal Investment

CHAPTER *4*

PASSIVE INCOME STRATEGIES THAT REQUIRE MINIMAL INVESTMENT

One strategy for generating passive income that requires minimal investment is creating an online course. While developing a course takes time and effort, the startup costs can be relatively low, especially compared to other passive income strategies like rental property or investing in stocks.

Another strategy is dividend investing. Dividend investing involves buying stocks that pay dividends, which are a portion of the company's earnings that are distributed to shareholders. While it does require an initial investment to purchase stocks, it can generate a steady stream of passive income over time.

Another way to generate passive income with minimal investment is through peer-to-peer lending. This involves lending money to individuals or businesses through online platforms, which then pay you back with interest. While there is some risk involved, as with any investment, it can be a way to generate passive income with minimal upfront costs.

Additionally, creating and selling digital products, such as eBooks or printables, can be a low-cost way to generate passive income. The initial investment may include purchasing design software or hiring a freelancer to create the product, but once created, it can be sold repeatedly without additional investment.

Another strategy is affiliate marketing, which involves promoting someone else's product and earning a commission on any resulting sales. While there may be some initial costs associated with building a website or social media presence, the investment is relatively low compared to other passive income strategies.

Renting out your possessions or your home through platforms like Airbnb or Turo can generate passive income with minimal investment. While there may be some costs associated with preparing your property for rental, such as cleaning or repairs, the potential for earning passive income can make it a worthwhile investment.

Another passive income strategy that requires minimal investment is investing in dividend-paying stocks. Dividend-paying stocks are shares of a company that distribute a portion of their earnings to shareholders in the form of dividends. By investing in these stocks, you can earn a regular income stream without having to sell the shares.

One thing that many people may not know about dividend-paying stocks is that they can be a relatively stable and consistent source of income. While stock prices can fluctuate, companies with a history of paying dividends tend to continue doing so, even during economic downturns.

Investing in dividend-paying stocks also provides the opportunity for long-term growth. By reinvesting the dividends you earn, you can buy more shares of the company, which can increase your overall returns over time.

Another strategy that requires minimal investment is peer-to-peer lending. This involves lending money to individuals or small businesses through online platforms, earning interest on the loan repayments. While there is a risk of default, many platforms offer ways to diversify your investment across multiple loans to reduce this risk.

A lesser-known strategy is creating and selling digital printables. Digital printables are downloadable files that can be printed at home, such as planner pages, calendars, or art prints. By creating and selling these digital products, you can earn passive income without the need for physical inventory or shipping.

Lastly, renting out a spare room or property on Airbnb can be a lucrative source of passive income. While there may be some initial costs associated with preparing the space for guests, renting it out regularly can provide a steady stream of income with relatively little ongoing effort. Additionally, by renting out a room or property, you may be able to deduct certain expenses on your taxes, such as cleaning fees or repairs.

Create a mobile app: If you have an idea for a mobile app, you can hire a developer to build it for you. Once the app is launched and available for download, you can generate passive income through advertising or by charging users for premium features.

Rent out your car: If you have a car that you don't use all the time, you can rent it out on platforms like Turo or Getaround. These platforms handle the logistics of renting your car, so all you have to do is sit back and collect the rental income.

Rent out a room in your home: If you have a spare room in your home, you can rent it out on Airbnb or other vacation rental platforms. You can make a significant amount of money by renting out a room on a short-term basis, and you can do it with minimal investment.

Invest in dividend-paying stocks: Investing in dividend-paying stocks can be an excellent way to generate passive income over the long term. By buying stocks in companies that pay dividends, you can earn regular payments without having to do any work.

Create a niche website: Creating a website focused on a particular niche can be an excellent way to generate passive income. By creating content that's valuable to your target audience, you can attract visitors to your site and monetize it through advertising, affiliate marketing, or other means.

Create an online course: If you have expertise in a particular area, you can create an online course and sell it on platforms like Udemy or Skillshare. Once you've created the course, you can continue to earn passive income from it for years to come.

Write an eBook: Writing an eBook can be a great way to generate passive income. Once you've written the book, you can publish it on Amazon or other eBook platforms and earn royalties on each sale.

Overall, there are many passive income strategies that require minimal investment. With a little creativity and effort, you can generate income streams that continue to pay off over time.

Create and sell printables: With a graphic design software, you can create digital files such as planners, calendars, art prints, and other downloadable templates, and sell them on platforms like Etsy, Gumroad, or your own website.

Invest in dividend-paying stocks: Dividend stocks are shares of companies that distribute a portion of their earnings to their shareholders regularly. By investing in dividend-paying stocks, you can earn passive income through regular dividend payments.

Write and self-publish e-books: If you have writing skills, you can write and self-publish e-books on platforms like Amazon Kindle Direct Publishing or Smashwords. Once you've published your book, it can earn you passive income for years to come.

Create and sell online courses: If you have expertise in a particular area, you can create and sell online courses on platforms like Udemy, Skillshare, or Teachable. Once you've created your course, it can earn you passive income as long as it remains relevant and valuable.

Rent out a spare room on Airbnb: If you have an extra room in your home, you can rent it out on Airbnb and earn passive income from guests who book your space.

Invest in real estate crowdfunding: Real estate crowdfunding platforms like Fundrise and RealtyMogul allow you to invest in real estate projects with as little as $500. You can earn passive income from rental income or from the appreciation of the property over time.

Create and sell a digital product: Digital products like software, plugins, and templates can be created and sold on platforms like CodeCanyon or Creative Market. Once you've created your product, it can earn you passive income for years to come.

These are just a few examples of passive income strategies that require minimal investment. With some time, effort, and creativity, anyone can start building passive income streams that can help them achieve financial freedom.

Investing in dividend-paying stocks

Investing in dividend-paying stocks is a popular passive income strategy, but many people may not be aware of the nuances and potential benefits involved. Here are some key points to consider:

Dividends are payouts made by companies to their shareholders, usually out of their profits. Dividend-paying stocks are those that have a track record of regularly paying dividends to their shareholders.

Dividend-paying stocks can provide a reliable stream of passive income, as long as the company maintains its dividend payments. It's important to research the company's financial health and dividend history before investing.

Dividend-paying stocks can also offer potential capital gains, as the stock price may increase over time. This can provide an additional source of passive income if the investor decides to sell their shares.

Investors can choose to reinvest their dividends by buying more shares of the company, which can lead to compounding returns over time.

Some dividend-paying stocks may offer higher yields than others, but higher yields may also indicate higher risk. It's important to consider the company's financial stability and potential for growth when evaluating dividend-paying stocks.

Investing in dividend-paying stocks requires some level of research and due diligence, as well as a long-term investment horizon. It may not be the best strategy for those looking for quick or guaranteed returns.

Overall, investing in dividend-paying stocks can be a rewarding passive income strategy for those who are willing to do their research and take a long-term approach to investing.

One important thing to note when it comes to investing in dividend-paying stocks is that not all dividends are equal. Some companies pay higher dividends than others, but high dividends don't always indicate a good investment. It's important to research a company's financial health and stability, as well as its track record of consistently paying dividends, before investing.

Another factor to consider is taxes. Dividend income is subject to taxes, and the tax rate can vary depending on factors such as your income level and how long you've held the stock. It's important to consult with a financial advisor or tax professional to understand the tax implications of investing in dividend-paying stocks.

Additionally, investors should be aware of the risks associated with any stock investment, including the potential for the stock price to decline, the possibility of a company reducing or suspending its dividend payments, and the potential for market volatility.

Overall, investing in dividend-paying stocks can be a good way to generate passive income over the long term, but it's important to do your research and make informed investment decisions based on your financial goals and risk tolerance.

Look at the dividend payout ratio: This is the percentage of earnings that a company pays out as dividends. A high payout ratio could mean that the company may not be reinvesting enough profits into the business for future growth. Conversely, a very low payout ratio could mean that the company is retaining too much cash that could otherwise be paid out as dividends.

Consider the dividend yield: This is the percentage of the stock price that the annual dividend payment represents. However, it's important to note that a high dividend yield isn't always a good thing. A company with an unsustainably high yield may be forced to cut its dividend in the future.

Look at the company's history of dividend payments: A company with a long history of paying dividends is generally considered more stable and reliable. It's also worth looking at how the company has increased its dividends over time, as this can be a sign of a healthy business that is able to continue to pay out more to shareholders.

Diversify your portfolio: Just like with any other type of investment, it's important to diversify your portfolio when it comes to dividend-paying stocks. Investing in a variety of companies across different sectors can help to reduce risk and increase potential returns.

Be mindful of taxes: Dividend income is generally taxed at a lower rate than other types of investment income, but it's still important to be mindful of tax implications when investing in dividend-paying stocks. Holding dividend-paying stocks in a tax-advantaged account, such as an IRA or 401(k), can help to minimize taxes on this type of income.

Peer-to-peer lending

Peer-to-peer lending (P2P lending) is a form of lending that allows individuals to lend money to other individuals or businesses without the need for a traditional financial institution like a bank. P2P lending has become increasingly popular in recent years, as it offers borrowers the opportunity to access funds at lower interest rates than traditional loans and investors the opportunity to earn higher returns on their money.

One thing many people may not know about P2P lending is that it typically involves a platform or website that connects borrowers with lenders. These platforms often have their own set of rules and regulations for lending and borrowing, which can vary depending on the platform.

Another important aspect of P2P lending is that it involves risk, just like any other form of investment. Borrowers may default on their loans, which means lenders could lose their investment. Therefore, it is important for investors to carefully assess the risk associated with each loan before making an investment.

It is also important to note that P2P lending may not be available in all countries or regions, as it is subject to local laws and regulations. Additionally, there may be restrictions on who can participate as a borrower or lender, such as minimum income or credit score requirements.

Finally, P2P lending may not be as liquid as other forms of investments, as lenders typically have to wait until the loan is repaid to receive their money back. This means that investors should be prepared to hold onto their investments for an extended period of time.

Peer-to-peer lending, also known as P2P lending, is a popular way to earn passive income. However, there are some things that many people do not know about this investment strategy.

One thing to keep in mind is that P2P lending involves lending money to individual borrowers, and there is always a risk that the borrower may default on the loan. This means that there is a risk of losing some or all of the money that you have invested. It is important to carefully research the lending platform and the borrowers before investing any money.

Another important consideration is the potential returns. While P2P lending can be a great way to earn passive income, the returns are generally not as high as other investment strategies, such as dividend-paying stocks or rental properties.

It is also important to note that P2P lending may not be suitable for everyone. Some lending platforms may require a minimum investment, and there may be restrictions on who can invest. Additionally, P2P lending is not regulated in the same way that traditional banking and investment products are, which means that there is no guarantee of returns or protection in the event of fraud or default.

Despite these considerations, P2P lending can be a viable passive income strategy for those who are willing to take on some risk and do their research. With careful selection of lending platforms and borrowers, investors can potentially earn consistent returns over time.

Borrowers and investors are matched through a platform: Peer-to-peer lending platforms connect borrowers with investors who are willing to lend money. These platforms use algorithms and other technologies to match borrowers with investors based on their creditworthiness and risk profile.

Loans are unsecured: Unlike traditional bank loans, peer-to-peer loans are typically unsecured, meaning that they are not backed by collateral. This means that borrowers are not required to put up assets as collateral in case they default on the loan.

Borrowers may have lower credit scores: Many peer-to-peer lending platforms cater to borrowers who may have lower credit scores and may not qualify for traditional bank loans. However, these borrowers may be charged higher interest rates to compensate for the higher risk.

Investors can diversify their portfolio: Peer-to-peer lending offers investors the opportunity to diversify their investment portfolio beyond traditional stocks and bonds. By investing in multiple loans with different risk profiles, investors can spread their risk and potentially earn higher returns.

There are risks involved: While peer-to-peer lending can be a lucrative investment opportunity, it is not without risks. Investors may face the risk of default if borrowers are unable to repay their loans, and there is no guarantee of returns. It is important for investors to carefully research the platform and the loans before investing and to diversify their portfolio to minimize risk.

Peer-to-peer lending, also known as P2P lending, is a form of alternative investing that has gained popularity in recent years. It involves individuals lending money to other individuals or businesses through an online platform, without the involvement of traditional financial institutions like banks.

One thing that many people may not know about P2P lending is that it can offer higher returns than traditional forms of investing like stocks and bonds. The reason for this is that investors can earn interest rates that are often much higher than those offered by savings accounts and CDs, and can also diversify their investments across multiple borrowers.

However, it is important to note that P2P lending also comes with its risks. The loans are typically unsecured, meaning there is no collateral to back them up, and borrowers may default on their payments. Additionally, P2P lending platforms are not regulated in the same way that traditional financial institutions are, which means that investors need to be cautious when selecting which platform to use.

Another important thing to keep in mind is that P2P lending is not without fees. While some platforms charge no fees for investors, others charge fees for loan origination, servicing, or late payments. Investors should carefully consider these fees when selecting a platform to use.

Overall, P2P lending can be a great way to earn passive income, but it is important to carefully evaluate the risks and fees associated with each platform before investing.

Investing in real estate crowdfunding

Real estate crowdfunding is a relatively new investment opportunity that allows investors to pool their funds together to invest in real estate projects. This can be an attractive option for those looking to invest in real estate without the high capital requirements of traditional real estate investing. Here are some things many people may not know about real estate crowdfunding:

Increased Access to Real Estate Deals: Real estate crowdfunding provides investors with access to real estate deals that they may not have been able to invest in otherwise. This includes deals in different geographies, property types, and investment strategies.

Diversification: Real estate crowdfunding allows investors to diversify their portfolio by investing in different real estate projects. This can help to reduce risk and increase potential returns.

Reduced Barriers to Entry: Traditional real estate investing typically requires a high capital investment, making it difficult for many people to participate. Real estate crowdfunding, on the other hand, often has lower investment minimums, making it more accessible to a wider range of investors.

Less Hands-On Involvement: Real estate crowdfunding allows investors to invest in real estate projects without the hands-on involvement that comes with traditional real estate investing. This means that investors can earn passive income without having to deal with the day-to-day responsibilities of property management.

Crowdfunding Risks: As with any investment, there are risks associated with real estate crowdfunding. Some of these risks include project delays, changes in market conditions, and the potential for the project to fail. It's important for investors to do their due diligence and carefully evaluate the risks associated with each investment opportunity.

Fees: Real estate crowdfunding platforms charge fees for their services, such as platform fees and servicing fees. These fees can vary depending on the platform and investment opportunity, so it's important for investors to carefully evaluate the costs associated with each investment opportunity.

Limited Liquidity: Real estate crowdfunding investments are generally illiquid, meaning that they cannot be easily sold or traded. Investors should be prepared to hold their investment for the duration of the project or until a liquidity event occurs.

Overall, real estate crowdfunding can be a viable option for those looking to invest in real estate with a lower capital investment and less hands-on involvement. However, as with any investment, it's important for investors to do their due diligence and carefully evaluate the risks and potential returns associated with each investment opportunity.

Another thing that people may not know about real estate crowdfunding is the potential for diversification. With traditional real estate investments, investors typically need to purchase an entire property or unit, which can be expensive and limit their ability to diversify their portfolio. However, with real estate crowdfunding, investors can invest in a variety of properties and projects with smaller amounts of capital, allowing for greater diversification.

It's also worth noting that real estate crowdfunding is not without its risks. Like any investment, there is always a chance of losing money, and investors should thoroughly research and understand the risks before investing. Additionally, some platforms may have fees and restrictions that could impact returns, so it's important to carefully review the terms and conditions before investing.

It's important to choose a reputable real estate crowdfunding platform. Investors should research the platform's track record, management team, and fees, as well as any regulatory oversight or accreditation.

Real estate crowdfunding has become an increasingly popular way for investors to get involved in real estate without having to put up the large amounts of capital typically required for direct property ownership. However, there are some aspects of real estate crowdfunding that many people may not be aware of:

Limited liquidity: Unlike publicly traded stocks or bonds, real estate crowdfunding investments can be illiquid, meaning it may be difficult to sell them quickly if you need to access your funds.

Diversification: Real estate crowdfunding can be a way to diversify your investment portfolio beyond traditional stocks and bonds, but it's important to do your due diligence and research the platforms and investments you're considering to ensure they align with your risk tolerance and financial goals.

Fees: Real estate crowdfunding platforms often charge fees for their services, such as management fees and performance fees. It's important to read the fine print and understand these fees before investing.

Risk: As with any investment, there is always risk involved in real estate crowdfunding. Investments can lose value, and there is a risk that the underlying property may not perform as expected.

Regulation: Real estate crowdfunding is regulated by the Securities and Exchange Commission (SEC) and is subject to certain rules and regulations. It's important to understand these regulations and ensure that the platform you're using is compliant.

Overall, real estate crowdfunding can be a viable option for investors looking to diversify their portfolios and potentially earn passive income from real estate investments. However, it's important to do your research and understand the potential risks and limitations before investing.

Renting out a room on Airbnb

Renting out a room on Airbnb has become a popular way to earn passive income, but there are some things many people may not know about this strategy.

Firstly, it's important to note that Airbnb has certain rules and regulations that hosts must follow, including local laws and taxes. It's important to check with your local government to ensure you are following all necessary regulations.

Another thing to consider is the time and effort it takes to manage an Airbnb rental. As a host, you'll need to communicate with guests, clean the room or space, and provide amenities such as toiletries, clean linens, and towels. This can be time-consuming, and it's important to factor in the cost of your time when considering the potential profitability of this strategy.

Additionally, it's important to note that there may be some risks involved with renting out your space to strangers. It's a good idea to screen guests carefully and to have a clear cancellation policy in case of any issues that arise.

Lastly, it's important to consider the potential wear and tear on your space. Depending on the length of the rental and the type of guests you attract, there may be some damage to your property or belongings. It's important to set clear rules and guidelines for your guests to minimize any potential damage.

Overall, renting out a room on Airbnb can be a great way to earn passive income, but it's important to carefully consider the potential risks and responsibilities involved.

Hosts can set their own prices: One advantage of listing a room on Airbnb is that hosts can set their own prices, based on demand, season, and local events. Hosts can also choose to offer discounts or special rates for longer stays.

Cleaning and maintenance costs: It's important for hosts to factor in cleaning and maintenance costs when setting their rental prices. Depending on the frequency of rentals, hosts may need to hire a professional cleaning service to ensure the room is ready for the next guest.

Legal and tax considerations: Hosts need to be aware of local laws and regulations around short-term rentals, including zoning laws, building codes, and taxes. Hosts may need to obtain permits or licenses to legally rent out a room on Airbnb.

Safety concerns: Hosts should take precautions to ensure the safety of their guests, such as installing smoke detectors, providing emergency contact information, and securing valuables. Hosts may also want to consider liability insurance in case of accidents or injuries.

Time commitment: Renting out a room on Airbnb can be time-consuming, especially if hosts are handling everything themselves. Hosts need to be prepared to communicate with guests, handle reservations and payments, and coordinate check-in and check-out times. Some hosts choose to hire a property management company to handle these tasks for them.

Reviews and reputation: Reviews are a key part of Airbnb's reputation-based system. Hosts who consistently receive positive reviews are more likely to attract future guests, while hosts with negative reviews may struggle to fill their rental. Hosts need to be responsive to guest feedback and take steps to address any issues that arise during a rental.

One thing that many people may not know about renting out a room on Airbnb is the potential legal and regulatory considerations that may apply. Depending on where you live, there may be local laws and regulations governing short-term rentals, which can include things like permits, taxes, and safety requirements. It's important to research and understand these requirements before listing your space on Airbnb to avoid potential legal issues or penalties.

Additionally, it's important to note that hosting on Airbnb requires a significant amount of time and effort to manage, such as responding to inquiries, preparing the room for guests, and maintaining the space during the guest's stay. This can be challenging if you have a busy schedule or are not able to be present during the guest's stay.

Finally, while renting out a room on Airbnb can be a lucrative source of passive income, it is important to be aware of the risks involved. This can include potential damage to your property, liability for accidents or injuries that occur during the guest's stay, and the potential for negative reviews that could impact your future bookings. It's important to carefully weigh these factors before deciding to rent out your space on Airbnb.

Starting a blog and monetizing it

Starting a blog and monetizing it is a popular passive income strategy that has become increasingly accessible with the rise of platforms like WordPress and Blogger. Here are some things that many people may not know about this strategy:

Building an audience takes time: Starting a blog and earning a significant income from it is not a quick or easy process. It can take months or even years of consistent effort to build up a large enough audience to generate significant revenue.

There are many ways to monetize a blog: While many people think of advertising and sponsorships as the primary ways to monetize a blog, there are actually many other ways to earn passive income from a blog. These can include affiliate marketing, selling digital products or courses, offering consulting services, and more.

Quality content is key: The success of a blog largely depends on the quality of its content. In order to attract and retain an audience, it's important to consistently produce high-quality, engaging content that provides value to readers.

SEO is important: Search engine optimization (SEO) is a critical component of building a successful blog. By optimizing your blog for search engines, you can increase your visibility and attract more traffic to your site.

Building an email list is crucial: One of the most effective ways to monetize a blog is by building an email list. By collecting the email addresses of your readers, you can stay in touch with them and promote your products or services on an ongoing basis.

It's important to diversify your income streams: Relying solely on one source of income from your blog can be risky. It's important to diversify your income streams by exploring multiple ways to monetize your blog, such as through affiliate marketing, selling products or courses, offering consulting services, and more.

Starting a blog can be a great way to generate passive income, but it requires a lot of work and patience to build a successful blog that generates consistent income. Here are some things that many people may not know about starting a blog and monetizing it:

Choosing a niche: It's important to choose a niche for your blog that you are passionate about and can write about consistently. Choosing a popular niche can also increase the chances of your blog being successful.

Creating high-quality content: Creating high-quality content that adds value to your readers is essential to the success of your blog. It's important to write in a way that is engaging, informative, and easy to read.

Building an audience: Building an audience takes time and effort. You can do this by promoting your blog on social media, guest posting on other blogs, and commenting on other blogs in your niche.

Monetizing your blog: There are several ways to monetize your blog, including:

Advertising: You can place ads on your blog and earn money every time someone clicks on them.

Affiliate marketing: You can promote products or services on your blog and earn a commission on any sales made through your unique affiliate link.

Sponsored content: You can work with brands to create sponsored content on your blog.

Selling digital products: You can create and sell your own digital products, such as e-books, courses, and printables.

Consistency is key: To be successful with blogging, consistency is key. It's important to publish new content on a regular basis and engage with your audience through comments and social media.

Overall, starting a blog can be a great way to generate passive income, but it takes time, effort, and patience to build a successful blog that generates consistent income.

It's not a get-rich-quick scheme: While it's possible to make a significant amount of money through blogging, it's not an overnight success. It requires patience, consistency, and hard work to build a successful blog that generates a sustainable income.

Building an audience is essential: In order to monetize a blog, you need to have a significant following. This means creating valuable content, promoting your blog through social media, guest posting, and other means to attract readers and build your audience.

Monetization methods go beyond ads: While displaying ads on your blog can be a way to generate income, there are many other ways to monetize a blog, such as affiliate marketing, sponsored posts, selling digital products, and offering services.

It's important to diversify income streams: Relying solely on one income stream can be risky. Bloggers should consider diversifying their income streams by exploring different monetization methods, such as selling digital products or offering services.

It's important to disclose sponsored content: If a blogger is being paid to endorse a product or service, they must disclose that it is sponsored content. Failure to do so could damage their reputation and result in legal consequences.

Collaboration can be beneficial: Collaborating with other bloggers, brands, or influencers can be a way to expand your reach, attract new readers, and increase your income potential.

SEO is critical: Search engine optimization (SEO) can make a significant impact on a blog's visibility and success. Bloggers should focus on creating quality content and optimizing it for search engines to attract organic traffic.

Consistency is key: Regularly publishing high-quality content is essential for building and maintaining an engaged audience. Bloggers should strive to create a content schedule and stick to it.

The blogging landscape is constantly changing: Bloggers should stay up-to-date with industry trends, changes in algorithms, and new monetization methods to stay competitive and relevant.

Building relationships is crucial: Engaging with your audience, networking with other bloggers, and building relationships with brands and potential clients can all help grow your blog and increase your income potential.

PART 4

Passive Income Strategies for the Creative Entrepreneur

CHAPTER 5

PASSIVE INCOME STRATEGIES FOR THE CREATIVE ENTREPRENEUR

Passive income strategies for the creative entrepreneur can be a great way to earn money while doing what you love. Here are some lesser-known tips and ideas:

Licensing your creative work: If you're a graphic designer, artist, or musician, you can earn passive income by licensing your work. This means you can get paid for every use of your artwork, music, or other creative work, without having to actively create new pieces. For example, you can license your designs to be used on t-shirts, mugs, and other products.

Creating digital assets: Consider creating digital assets such as templates, graphics, and other design elements that others can purchase and use for their own projects. You can create these assets once and sell them over and over again.

Building a community: By building a community around your creative work, you can attract sponsors and advertisers who want to reach your audience. You can monetize your blog or social media accounts through sponsored posts or affiliate marketing.

Teaching your skills: If you have a skill that others want to learn, consider creating an online course or writing an e-book that teaches others how to do what you do. This can be a great way to earn passive income while helping others.

Selling merchandise: If you have a strong personal brand, you can sell merchandise such as t-shirts, stickers, and other items with your logo or artwork on them. You can set up an online store and fulfill orders through a print-on-demand service, which means you don't have to keep inventory on hand.

Overall, it's important to remember that building a passive income stream takes time and effort, but it can be well worth it in the long run. By leveraging your creative skills and building a community around your work, you can earn money while doing what you love.

Print-on-Demand Products: You can create designs for t-shirts, mugs, stickers, phone cases, and other items and upload them to print-on-demand platforms like Redbubble, Teespring, and Society6. Whenever someone purchases an item with your design, you earn a royalty fee.

Stock Photography: If you have a passion for photography, you can sell your photos as stock images on websites like Shutterstock, iStock, and Adobe Stock. Every time someone downloads your photo, you earn a commission.

Creating and Selling Fonts: If you're skilled in typography, you can create and sell your own fonts on websites like MyFonts and Fontspring. You earn a commission every time someone purchases your font.

Licensing Your Music: If you're a musician, you can earn passive income by licensing your music for use in commercials, TV shows, movies, and video games. Platforms like Musicbed and AudioJungle allow you to upload your music and earn royalties every time it's licensed.

Digital Art: If you're an artist, you can create and sell digital art pieces on platforms like OpenSea and SuperRare. You earn a commission every time someone purchases one of your pieces.

Online Courses: If you're an expert in a particular field, you can create an online course and sell it on platforms like Udemy,

Skillshare, and Coursera. You earn passive income every time someone enrolls in your course.

Writing E-Books: If you're a skilled writer, you can write and self-publish e-books on platforms like Amazon Kindle Direct Publishing. You earn a royalty fee every time someone purchases your book.

These are just a few additional passive income strategies for the creative entrepreneur that you may not have known about. With the rise of digital technology, there are many more opportunities to monetize your creative skills and earn passive income.

Creating a mobile app

Creating a mobile app can be a great way to generate passive income, but there are some important things to consider before diving in. Here are a few things that many people may not know:

It can be expensive: Creating a high-quality mobile app can require a significant investment of time and money. You may need to hire developers, designers, and other professionals to help bring your vision to life. Additionally, ongoing maintenance and updates can also be costly.

You need to do your research: Before creating an app, it's important to do your market research to make sure there's demand for your idea. You'll also need to research your competition and figure out how to make your app stand out in a crowded marketplace.

Monetization strategies vary: There are a variety of ways to monetize a mobile app, including in-app purchases, subscription models, and advertising. You'll need to decide which strategy is right for your app and your target audience.

App store optimization is crucial: Once your app is created, it's important to optimize it for the app stores to maximize visibility and downloads. This includes things like choosing the right keywords, creating a compelling app description, and providing high-quality screenshots and videos.

User feedback is essential: Your app is only as good as your users think it is, so it's important to solicit feedback and make improvements based on user suggestions. Regular updates and bug fixes can help keep users engaged and increase the likelihood of positive reviews and word-of-mouth marketing.

It can be costly: While there are many app development tools available, creating a quality mobile app can still be a costly endeavor, especially if you plan to outsource the development to professionals. You may also need to budget for ongoing maintenance and updates to keep your app relevant and functional.

Monetizing can be challenging: While there are many ways to monetize a mobile app, such as in-app purchases, subscriptions, and advertisements, it can be challenging to make a significant income from your app. The app market is highly competitive, and users may be hesitant to spend money on a new app, especially if there are similar free alternatives available.

App stores take a cut: If you plan to distribute your app through app stores such as Google Play or the Apple App Store, keep in mind that they take a percentage of your earnings. For example, Google takes a 30% cut of all in-app purchases made through Google Play.

Marketing is crucial: Even if you have a great app, it won't make money if people don't know about it. Marketing is essential to get your app in front of potential users, and it can be a time-consuming and costly process.

App development is a constantly evolving field: To create a successful mobile app, you need to stay up-to-date with the latest trends and technologies in app development. This can require ongoing education and learning, which can be a challenge for some entrepreneurs.

Overall, creating a mobile app can be a lucrative passive income strategy, but it requires significant time, effort, and investment. It's important to do your research and have a solid plan before jumping into app development.

Designing and selling custom merchandise

Designing and selling custom merchandise is a popular way for creative entrepreneurs to generate passive income. However, there are some things that many people may not know about this strategy.

One thing to keep in mind is the importance of choosing the right platform to sell your merchandise. There are many options available, from marketplaces like Etsy and Redbubble to custom storefronts like Shopify. Each platform has its own strengths and weaknesses, and it's important to choose one that aligns with your goals and target audience.

Another consideration is the importance of creating a strong brand and unique designs. With so much competition in the marketplace, it's essential to stand out with a distinctive style and brand identity that resonates with your target audience.

In addition, it's important to understand the costs involved in creating and selling custom merchandise. This includes not only the cost of materials and production, but also the fees charged by the platform you choose to sell on. It's important to factor in these costs when pricing your products to ensure that you're making a profit.

It's worth noting that creating and selling custom merchandise requires ongoing effort and attention. This includes creating new designs, promoting your products, and staying up to date with the latest trends and best practices in the industry. While it can be a rewarding way to generate passive income, it's not a "set it and forget it" strategy, and it requires ongoing investment in time and resources to be successful.

Custom merchandise refers to products that are created with unique designs or artwork. These products can be anything from t-shirts, mugs, phone cases, tote bags, stickers, and more. One way to make passive income through custom merchandise is by designing your own products and selling them online.

Here are some things many people do not know about designing and selling custom merchandise:

Print-on-Demand Services: You don't need to stock up inventory when designing and selling custom merchandise. Print-on-demand services allow you to create designs that are then printed on-demand on the products you choose, only after a customer has placed an order. This means you don't have to invest in inventory upfront, and you also don't have to handle the shipping and fulfillment process.

Niche Markets: You can target niche markets when designing and selling custom merchandise. For instance, if you're a graphic designer and specialize in creating designs related to a specific industry or interest, you can create products that cater to that specific market.

Multiple Platforms: There are several online platforms where you can sell your custom merchandise, including Etsy, Redbubble, Teespring, and Amazon Merch. Each platform has its own set of rules and fees, so it's important to research and compare the options to find the best fit for your business.

Branding: It's important to have a strong brand identity when designing and selling custom merchandise. This includes a cohesive design style, a unique brand voice, and a clear message that resonates with your target audience. Your branding should help you stand out from competitors and connect with customers on a deeper level.

Licensing: If you create designs that incorporate copyrighted material, you may need to obtain a license to use that material legally. For example, if you create a design featuring a character from a popular TV show, you may need to obtain a license from the show's creators to use that character in your design. Failing to obtain the proper licenses can result in legal action, so it's important to research the legal requirements and obtain the necessary permissions before selling your custom merchandise.

Monetizing your YouTube channel

Monetizing a YouTube channel has become a popular way to earn passive income. Here are some things that many people may not know about:

Eligibility: Before you can monetize your YouTube channel, you must meet the eligibility criteria, which includes having at least 1,000 subscribers and 4,000 watch hours in the past 12 months.

Ad formats: YouTube offers several ad formats that creators can use to monetize their content, including display ads, overlay ads, skippable video ads, non-skippable video ads, and sponsored cards.

YouTube Partner Program: To monetize your content, you must join the YouTube Partner Program. This program allows creators to monetize their videos through ads, memberships, and merchandise sales.

Revenue share: Creators earn a portion of the revenue generated from ads on their videos. The revenue share is typically 55% for the creator and 45% for YouTube.

Other revenue streams: In addition to ads, creators can earn money from YouTube through memberships, merchandise sales, and Super Chat, which allows fans to pay to have their messages highlighted during live streams.

Brand deals: Creators can also earn money through brand deals, where they promote a product or service in their videos in exchange for payment.

Content ID: YouTube's Content ID system allows creators to monetize videos that contain copyrighted material. If a creator's video is flagged for copyright infringement, they can either remove the offending material or allow ads to appear on the video and share the revenue with the copyright owner.

Analytics: YouTube provides creators with analytics data that can help them understand their audience and optimize their content for maximum revenue potential.

Community guidelines: Creators must follow YouTube's community guidelines, which prohibit content that is violent, hateful, sexually explicit, or promotes dangerous activities.

Ad revenue is just one source of income: While ad revenue is a common way for YouTubers to earn money, there are other ways to monetize your channel. For example, you can create sponsored content, sell merchandise, or even offer paid memberships to your viewers.

Your niche matters: Different niches will have different opportunities for monetization. For example, channels that focus on beauty or fashion may have more opportunities for sponsored content, while channels that focus on technology may have more opportunities for affiliate marketing.

Consistency is key: If you want to monetize your YouTube channel, you need to consistently create high-quality content that resonates with your audience. This will help you build a loyal following, which is crucial for monetization.

You need to have a certain number of subscribers and watch time: To be eligible for monetization on YouTube, you need to have at least 1,000 subscribers and 4,000 hours of watch time within the past 12 months.

YouTube takes a cut of your earnings: YouTube takes a 45% cut of the ad revenue generated by your videos. This means that if you earn $100 from ads, YouTube will take $45 and you will receive $55.

There are different types of ads: There are different types of ads that can appear on your videos, including display ads, overlay ads, and sponsored cards. Each type of ad has different requirements and payment structures.

Engagement is important: The more engagement your videos have (i.e. likes, comments, shares), the more likely they are to be recommended to other viewers. This can lead to more views and more monetization opportunities.

You can use analytics to improve your earnings: YouTube provides a wealth of analytics data that you can use to improve your videos and increase your earnings. For example, you can see which videos are getting the most views and engagement, and use this information to create more content that resonates with your audience.

Selling stock photography

Selling stock photography can be a great way to generate passive income for photographers, but there are some things that many people may not know about this strategy. Here are a few things to keep in mind:

Quality is key: In order to be successful selling stock photography, you need to have high-quality images. This means that you need to have a good eye for composition, lighting, and subject matter. You also need to ensure that your images are technically sound, with proper exposure, focus, and color balance.

Research the market: Before you start selling your stock photos, it's important to do your research and find out what types of images are in demand. Look at the top-selling images on stock photography sites and try to understand why they are popular. This will help you to create images that have a better chance of selling.

Choose the right platform: There are many different platforms for selling stock photography, including Shutterstock, Adobe Stock, and Getty Images. Each platform has its own requirements and commission rates, so it's important to do your research and choose the one that best suits your needs.

Be prepared to submit a lot of images: Selling stock photography is a numbers game, so you need to be prepared to submit a lot of images in order to make a significant income. However, don't sacrifice quality for quantity – it's better to have a smaller portfolio of high-quality images than a large portfolio of mediocre ones.

Understand the licensing agreements: When you sell stock photography, you are essentially licensing your images for use by others. It's important to understand the terms of the licensing agreements, including the duration of the license, the permitted uses of the image, and any restrictions on the image's use.

Keep track of your earnings: Finally, it's important to keep track of your earnings from stock photography so that you can accurately report them on your taxes. Many stock photography platforms provide detailed earnings reports that make this task easier, but you should also keep your own records just in case.

Stock photography is a popular way to generate passive income for photographers and non-photographers alike. However, there are some lesser-known aspects of this field that can affect your success as a stock photographer:

Quality matters: While there are many stock photography websites that accept just about any photo, if you want to be successful and generate good passive income, you need to focus on taking high-quality photos that have commercial appeal. It's important to research what types of images are in demand and ensure that your photos meet those standards.

Licensing is important: Stock photography websites typically offer different types of licenses, including royalty-free and rights-managed licenses. Royalty-free licenses allow the buyer to use the image multiple times, while rights-managed licenses offer more control over how the image is used. As a stock photographer, it's important to understand the different licensing options and how they can affect your earnings.

Your subject matter matters: While there is a market for all types of stock photography, some subject matter is more popular than others. It's important to research the types of images that are in demand and try to create photos that fit those niches.

Consistency is key: To be successful in stock photography, you need to consistently create high-quality images that meet the demand of buyers. It's important to develop a consistent style and brand that buyers will recognize and come back to.

You need to be aware of copyright laws: When selling stock photography, you need to ensure that you have the right to sell the images you are offering. This means ensuring that you have model releases and property releases where necessary, and that you are not infringing on any trademarks or copyrighted materials.

Starting a podcast and monetizing it

Starting a podcast has become increasingly popular in recent years, with many people using it as a way to share their ideas, experiences, and expertise with a wider audience. Here are some things to keep in mind if you're considering starting a podcast and monetizing it:

Choose a niche: It's important to choose a specific topic or theme for your podcast, as this will help you stand out and attract a dedicated audience. Focus on a topic that you're passionate about and that has a built-in audience.

Create high-quality content: Your content is what will keep your listeners coming back for more, so it's important to create high-quality, engaging episodes. This means investing in good equipment, editing software, and spending time writing and researching your episodes.

Build an audience: Once you've launched your podcast, it's important to promote it to build an audience. Utilize social media, guest appearances on other podcasts, and word of mouth to get the word out. Building a loyal audience is key to monetizing your podcast.

Monetize your podcast: There are several ways to monetize your podcast, including sponsorships, affiliate marketing, merchandise sales, and crowdfunding. Sponsorships are the most common way to monetize a podcast, where companies pay you to promote their products or services during your episodes.

Consider building a brand: If your podcast becomes popular, you may want to consider building a brand around it. This could include creating a website, merchandise, and even live events. Building a strong brand can help you monetize your podcast in new and creative ways.

Keep it consistent: Consistency is key when it comes to podcasting. Make sure you release new episodes on a regular schedule to keep your audience engaged and interested.

Don't overlook the legalities: Finally, it's important to make sure you understand the legalities of podcasting, including copyright laws and regulations around advertising and sponsorships. Make sure you do your research and consult with legal professionals if necessary.

Building a loyal audience takes time: Don't expect to make money immediately after launching your podcast. Building a loyal audience takes time and consistent effort. It's important to focus on creating high-quality content and engaging with your listeners to keep them coming back.

Sponsorship deals aren't the only way to monetize: While sponsorship deals are a popular way to monetize a podcast, they're not the only option. You can also consider selling merchandise, offering premium content or memberships, or using affiliate marketing to earn revenue.

Choose the right hosting platform: Choosing the right hosting platform for your podcast can impact your ability to monetize it. Look for a hosting platform that offers features like dynamic ad insertion, which allows you to insert ads into older episodes of your podcast.

Take advantage of social media: Social media platforms like Twitter, Facebook, and Instagram are great places to promote your podcast and engage with your listeners. You can use these platforms to build a community around your podcast and promote your monetization strategies.

Don't overlook the importance of analytics: Analytics can help you understand how your listeners engage with your podcast and what types of content resonate with them. Use analytics to track your downloads, audience demographics, and listener engagement, so you can make informed decisions about your monetization strategy.

PART 5
Alternative Passive Income Strategies

CHAPTER **6**

ALTERNATIVE PASSIVE INCOME STRATEGIES

Alternative passive income strategies refer to income-generating activities that do not fit into traditional categories such as investing, real estate, or online business. Here are some alternative passive income strategies that many people may not know about:

Peer-to-Peer Car Sharing: Similar to Airbnb, peer-to-peer car sharing allows car owners to rent out their vehicles to people in need of a car. Platforms such as Turo and Getaround make it easy for car owners to list their vehicles for rent and earn passive income while they are not using their cars.

Vending Machines: Investing in vending machines can be a great way to earn passive income. Once you purchase and set up the machines, they can generate cash flow around the clock. Vending machines can be placed in high-traffic areas such as offices, gyms, and shopping malls.

ATM Machines: Owning an ATM machine can also be a passive income stream. ATM owners earn a small fee every time someone uses the machine. The key is to find a high-traffic location where people need access to cash.

Storage Units: Investing in storage units can be a lucrative passive income strategy. Once you purchase and set up the units, tenants pay a monthly fee to store their belongings. It is important to find a location with high demand for storage units and to maintain them properly.

Royalties: If you are a musician, writer, or artist, you can earn passive income from royalties. Royalties are payments made to a copyright owner for the use of their work. This can include income from streaming services, book sales, and licensing agreements.

Peer-to-Peer Lending: Peer-to-peer lending is a form of lending where borrowers can receive loans from individual investors rather than traditional financial institutions. Investors earn interest on their investments while borrowers receive loans at lower interest rates than they would from a bank.

Online Marketplaces: Online marketplaces such as Amazon, Etsy, and eBay offer opportunities to sell products online without the need to create your own website or storefront. You can source products from wholesalers, create your own designs, or sell digital products such as ebooks and courses.

Collectibles: Collectibles such as rare coins, stamps, and art can appreciate in value over time and provide a source of passive income. It is important to research and understand the market before investing in collectibles.

Cryptocurrency Staking: Cryptocurrency staking is the process of holding and supporting a cryptocurrency network by locking up a certain amount of tokens. In return, stakers earn rewards in the form of more cryptocurrency. It is important to understand the risks associated with investing in cryptocurrency before staking.

Licensing Intellectual Property: If you own a patent, trademark, or other intellectual property, you can earn passive income by licensing it to others. Licensing allows others to use your intellectual property in exchange for royalties or licensing fees. It is important to work with a lawyer to properly draft and negotiate licensing agreements.

Renting out your car: Similar to renting out your home or room on Airbnb, you can also rent out your car on platforms like Turo or

Getaround. This can be a great way to generate passive income if you have a vehicle that is not being used frequently.

Peer-to-peer car sharing: Another option in the sharing economy is peer-to-peer car sharing. Platforms like HyreCar allow you to rent out your car to drivers who need a vehicle for ride-sharing services like Uber or Lyft.

Investing in a business: Rather than starting your own business, you can also invest in someone else's business and receive a portion of the profits. This can be done through equity crowdfunding platforms like SeedInvest or Wefunder.

Renting out storage space: If you have extra storage space in your home or garage, you can rent it out to people who need extra storage on platforms like Neighbor or StoreAtMyHouse.

Investing in farmland: Investing in farmland can be a way to generate passive income through leasing the land to farmers or participating in crop-sharing agreements. Platforms like FarmTogether allow investors to invest in farmland and earn returns on their investment.

Investing in dividend-paying ETFs: Similar to investing in dividend-paying stocks, you can also invest in dividend-paying exchange-traded funds (ETFs). These funds invest in a basket of dividend-paying stocks, providing diversification and potentially higher returns.

Selling digital products on Etsy: In addition to physical products, Etsy also allows you to sell digital products like printables, digital art, and templates. These products can be created once and sold repeatedly, providing a passive income stream.

Investing in real estate investment trusts (REITs): REITs are companies that own and manage real estate properties and pay out a portion of their income to investors in the form of dividends. This allows investors to earn passive income from real estate without the hassle of owning and managing physical properties.

Investing in cryptocurrency: While cryptocurrency is not without risk, investing in cryptocurrencies like Bitcoin or Ethereum can potentially provide passive income through capital gains or staking rewards.

Renting out outdoor space: If you have a yard or outdoor space, you can rent it out for events like weddings or parties on platforms like Splacer or Peerspace.

Renting out your car

Renting out your car is a passive income strategy that allows you to make money from your vehicle when you're not using it. It's an alternative to traditional car rental companies and can be a great option for people who don't need to use their car every day. Here are some things that many people may not know about renting out their car:

There are different types of car-sharing platforms: There are several car-sharing platforms available, including Turo, Getaround, and HyreCar. Each platform operates differently, so it's important to research which one best fits your needs and preferences.

Insurance coverage varies: Most car-sharing platforms provide insurance coverage, but the coverage varies based on the platform and the state you live in. Some platforms may require you to have your own insurance, while others provide coverage while the car is being rented out.

Maintenance is important: Renting out your car means that it will be used more often than if it were just sitting in your garage. This means that you need to keep up with regular maintenance, such as oil changes and tire rotations, to ensure that it stays in good condition.

You can set your own prices: Car-sharing platforms usually allow owners to set their own prices for their vehicles. It's important to research the market to ensure that your prices are competitive and reasonable.

Communication is key: Clear communication with renters is important to ensure that the rental process goes smoothly. This includes setting expectations for pick-up and drop-off times, discussing any rules or restrictions for the use of the car, and addressing any concerns or issues that arise during the rental period.

You can make a significant amount of money: Renting out your car can be a lucrative source of passive income, especially if you live in a popular tourist destination or urban area with high demand for cars. Some car owners have reported making thousands of dollars per year by renting out their vehicles.

Peer-to-peer car sharing platforms: In addition to traditional car rental companies, there are also peer-to-peer car sharing platforms like Turo and Getaround that allow car owners to rent out their vehicles to individuals on a short-term basis. This can be a great way to earn some extra income if you have a car that you don't use frequently.

Insurance: Before renting out your car, it's important to check with your insurance provider to make sure that you're covered in case of an accident. Some insurance policies don't cover commercial use of a vehicle, so it's important to make sure that you have adequate coverage.

Maintenance and upkeep: Renting out your car can put additional wear and tear on the vehicle, so it's important to stay on top of regular maintenance and make sure that the car is in good working condition. This can help to avoid breakdowns and keep renters happy.

Location: The demand for rental cars can vary depending on where you live, so it's important to consider the location of your car when deciding whether or not to rent it out. If you live in a busy city or near an airport, there may be more demand for rental cars than in a more rural area.

Pricing: When setting your rental rates, it's important to consider the market and what other rental cars are available in your area. You don't want to price yourself out of the market, but you also don't want to undercut yourself and not earn as much as you could.

Rental agreements: It's important to have a clear rental agreement in place to protect yourself and your renters. This should include things like the rental period, rental rates, and any fees or charges that may be incurred if the car is damaged or returned late.

Renting out storage space

Renting out storage space can be a profitable passive income strategy, especially if you have extra space that is not being used. Here are some things that many people may not know about this strategy:

You don't have to own the property: You can rent out storage space even if you don't own the property. Many landlords are open to subletting a storage unit or garage to tenants who need additional space.

Consider zoning laws: Before renting out storage space, you need to make sure you are complying with local zoning laws. Some areas may require special permits or have restrictions on what types of activities can be conducted in residential areas.

Liability insurance is important: As the owner of the storage space, you could be liable for any damage or injuries that occur on the property. It's important to have liability insurance to protect yourself in case of any accidents or incidents.

Determine a fair price: When setting a price for your storage space, consider the size of the unit, the location, and any additional amenities you are offering. Research the market to see what other storage units in the area are charging to make sure you are offering a competitive rate.

Marketing is key: To find tenants, you need to market your storage space effectively. Consider using online platforms such as Craigslist, Facebook Marketplace, or storage rental websites to advertise your space. You can also put up flyers in local businesses or use word-of-mouth to spread the word.

Screen tenants: It's important to screen potential tenants carefully to make sure they are trustworthy and won't cause damage to your property. Consider conducting background checks and checking references before renting out your storage space.

Overall, renting out storage space can be a simple and effective way to generate passive income, as long as you take the time to do it right and follow local regulations.

You don't necessarily need to own a storage facility: You can also rent out extra storage space in your home, garage, or shed. This can be a good option for those who don't want to invest in a separate storage facility or don't have the space for one.

You can set your own terms: As a storage space owner, you have the ability to set your own rental terms, such as the length of the rental agreement, the frequency of payment, and the price of the rental. This means you can customize your rental business to your own needs and preferences.

Insurance is important: Renting out storage space comes with risks, such as damage to property, theft, or loss. It's important to have proper insurance coverage to protect yourself and your renters.

Marketing is key: To attract renters, you'll need to market your storage space. This can include creating a website or social media presence, posting ads on local classifieds or rental websites, or using word-of-mouth referrals.

Consider legal requirements: Depending on where you live, there may be legal requirements for renting out storage space, such as obtaining proper permits or licenses. Make sure to do your research and comply with any regulations in your area.

Investing in vending machines

Investing in vending machines can be a great passive income strategy. Vending machines can be found in many public places, such as schools, offices, airports, malls, and train stations, and they provide customers with convenient access to snacks and drinks.

One thing that many people may not know about vending machines is that there are different types of vending machines available. In addition to traditional snack and beverage vending machines, there are also machines that dispense items like personal care products, electronics, and even art. Investing in a vending machine that dispenses a unique item can help differentiate your business and increase profits.

Another important factor to consider when investing in vending machines is the location. High-traffic areas with a large number of potential customers can significantly increase the profitability of your vending machine business. However, it is important to obtain permission from property owners and follow local regulations before placing your vending machines.

Additionally, investing in vending machines can require a significant upfront investment, as vending machines can be expensive to purchase and require ongoing maintenance and restocking. However, the potential for passive income and long-term returns can make it a worthwhile investment. It is important to carefully research and plan your vending machine business before making any investment decisions.

The vending machine industry is growing: According to a report by Research and Markets, the global vending machine market is expected to reach over $50 billion by 2026, with a CAGR of over 14%. This indicates that the vending machine industry is growing rapidly, and there are opportunities for investors to earn passive income through this business.

Location is crucial: The location of the vending machine is a crucial factor that can determine the success or failure of the business. High-traffic areas such as shopping malls, airports, hospitals, and train stations are ideal locations for vending machines. When selecting a location, it is important to consider the demographics of the area, foot traffic, and competition.

Different types of vending machines: There are various types of vending machines, including snack and soda machines, coffee vending machines, healthy vending machines, and even vending machines that dispense electronics or books. Investing in a specific type of vending machine will depend on the location and target market.

Maintenance is necessary: Like any other machine, vending machines require maintenance and repair. It is important to have a maintenance plan in place to ensure the machines are always in good working condition. This may involve regular cleaning, restocking, and repairs when necessary.

Consider the upfront costs: Investing in vending machines requires upfront costs, including the purchase or lease of the machines, inventory, and any necessary permits and licenses. It is important to calculate the total costs and potential returns before investing in vending machines.

Work with a reputable vending machine company: To ensure success in the vending machine business, it is important to work with a reputable vending machine company. This can help with the selection of the right machines, maintenance, and even finding the ideal location for the machines.

Investing in billboard advertising

Investing in billboard advertising is a passive income strategy that involves purchasing or leasing a billboard space and then renting it out to advertisers. Here are some things that many people may not know about this strategy:

The cost of a billboard can vary widely depending on the location, size, and visibility of the billboard. In prime locations, such as busy highways or popular tourist destinations, the cost can be quite high, while in less desirable locations the cost may be lower.

Before investing in a billboard, it's important to research local zoning laws and regulations, as there may be restrictions on the placement and size of billboards in certain areas.

It's also important to consider the maintenance and upkeep costs associated with owning or leasing a billboard. This can include things like cleaning and repairs, as well as any necessary permits or inspections.

While renting out billboard space can be a lucrative passive income strategy, it's important to have a solid marketing and advertising plan in place to attract potential advertisers. This may involve networking with local businesses, reaching out to advertising agencies, or even creating your own advertising campaign to showcase the value of the billboard.

Investing in billboard advertising can be a long-term strategy, as leases typically run for several years. However, it's important to have a plan in place for what you will do with the billboard if the lease expires or if the advertising market shifts.

Overall, investing in billboard advertising can be a profitable passive income strategy for those willing to put in the upfront costs and ongoing maintenance, and who are able to attract advertisers to the space.

Creating an online store and dropshipping products

Creating an online store and dropshipping products is a popular way to start a business and generate passive income. With dropshipping, you can sell products without having to keep inventory, handle shipping, or deal with returns. Instead, you work with a supplier who ships the products directly to the customer on your behalf.

Many people don't realize that there are several important steps to follow when setting up an online store and dropshipping products. First, you need to choose a niche and research potential suppliers. It's important to choose a niche that you are interested in and that has a demand in the market.

Once you've chosen a niche and found suppliers, you need to set up your online store. This includes choosing a platform to use, such as Shopify or WooCommerce, and customizing your store with a design and branding that appeals to your target audience.

Next, you need to optimize your product listings and ensure that they are attractive, informative, and search engine optimized. You'll also need to set up payment processing and shipping methods.

One thing that many people don't know is that dropshipping can be a highly competitive industry, so it's important to continually monitor and optimize your online store. This includes testing different products, marketing strategies, and pricing to find what works best for your business.

It's also important to keep up with customer service and address any issues promptly. This can help you build a positive reputation and gain repeat customers.

Many people overlook the importance of marketing their online store and products. It's essential to have a solid marketing strategy that includes social media, email marketing, paid advertising, and search engine optimization to drive traffic to your store and generate sales.

Niche selection: When starting a dropshipping business, it's important to choose a niche that has a demand in the market. Instead of selecting a broad category, it's better to narrow down to a specific product or set of related products to focus on. This allows you to stand out from competitors and cater to a specific audience.

Building a brand: A dropshipping business can also benefit from building a brand identity. This includes creating a unique logo, designing a website, and establishing a social media presence. A well-designed and memorable brand can help create trust and credibility among potential customers.

Supplier selection: Selecting the right supplier is crucial to the success of a dropshipping business. It's important to research and evaluate potential suppliers for reliability, quality, and pricing. In addition, having multiple suppliers can provide a backup in case one supplier has issues.

Managing inventory: With a dropshipping business, you don't physically handle the inventory, but it's still important to keep track of stock levels. It's essential to have a system in place to monitor stock levels and to communicate with suppliers to avoid overselling or stockouts.

Customer service: While the supplier handles the shipping and fulfillment, it's important to provide excellent customer service to ensure customer satisfaction. This includes responding to inquiries promptly, resolving issues, and providing a positive buying experience.

Marketing and promotion: With the increasing popularity of dropshipping, it's important to develop effective marketing strategies to stand out from competitors. This includes utilizing social media, creating content marketing, and utilizing paid advertising methods such as Google Ads or Facebook Ads.

Managing finances: A dropshipping business requires financial management such as tracking expenses, pricing products competitively, and managing profit margins. It's essential to have a clear understanding of the financial aspects of the business to make informed decisions and ensure profitability.

Overall, starting a dropshipping business requires careful planning, execution, and management to ensure success. It's important to stay up-to-date with the latest trends and technologies to stay competitive and grow the business over time.

PART 6
Navigating the Challenges of Building Passive Income

CHAPTER *7*

NAVIGATING THE CHALLENGES OF BUILDING PASSIVE INCOME

Building passive income streams can be a great way to supplement your income and achieve financial freedom. However, there are challenges that come with building passive income that many people may not be aware of. Here are a few:

It takes time and effort: Building passive income streams takes time and effort. It's not something that happens overnight. You need to put in the work upfront to create the systems and processes that will generate income for you over time.

It requires ongoing maintenance: Passive income streams are not completely passive. You need to maintain them to ensure that they continue to generate income. This may involve things like updating content, managing inventory, or dealing with customer service issues.

It involves some degree of risk: Any investment or business venture involves some degree of risk. It's important to be aware of the risks involved in building passive income streams and to make informed decisions based on your risk tolerance.

You need to stay up-to-date with market trends: To be successful in building passive income streams, you need to stay up-to-date with market trends and changes in consumer behavior. This may involve investing in new technology or tools, or adapting your strategies to stay ahead of the curve.

It requires a long-term mindset: Building passive income streams requires a long-term mindset. You need to be patient and willing to invest in something that may not pay off immediately but has the potential to generate income for years to come.

It's important to diversify: Relying on a single passive income stream can be risky. It's important to diversify your income streams to protect yourself from the potential loss of income from a single source.

You need to be disciplined with your money: Building passive income streams requires discipline with your money. You need to reinvest your profits into your business or investment portfolio to continue growing your passive income streams over time.

Overall, building passive income streams can be a great way to achieve financial freedom, but it's important to be aware of the challenges and risks involved and to approach it with a long-term mindset and disciplined approach.

One thing that many people may not realize is that building passive income streams can take time and effort. While the end goal is to have income coming in without having to put in active work, getting to that point can require a significant investment of time and energy.

Additionally, it's important to remember that not all passive income strategies will work for everyone. Each individual has unique strengths, skills, and resources, and what works for one person may not work for another. It's important to carefully consider your own situation and choose passive income strategies that align with your strengths and interests.

Another challenge to building passive income is the potential for market fluctuations and changes in demand. For example, if you invest in dividend-paying stocks, the value of those stocks may go down or the company may cut its dividend payouts. If you rely on rental income from a property, you may experience periods of vacancy or have difficult tenants. It's important to have a plan in place for these potential challenges and to diversify your passive income streams to reduce risk.

Finally, it's important to recognize that building passive income streams requires discipline and consistency. It's not enough to simply set up a passive income stream and expect it to generate income without any further effort. You may need to continually market your products or services, invest in new opportunities, or adjust your strategy to stay ahead of the curve. However, with patience and persistence, building passive income can be a rewarding and lucrative endeavor.

Overcoming the fear of failure

Overcoming the fear of failure is a common challenge that many people face when trying to build passive income. The fear of failure can prevent people from taking risks and pursuing their dreams, which can hold them back from achieving their goals.

One thing many people do not know is that failure is a natural part of the learning process. Everyone experiences failure at some point in their lives, and it is often through these failures that we learn and grow the most. It is important to recognize that failure does not define us, and that we can always learn from our mistakes and improve.

Another important aspect of overcoming the fear of failure is shifting our mindset. Instead of focusing on the negative consequences of failure, we can choose to see it as an opportunity to learn and improve. By reframing failure as a learning experience, we can reduce the emotional impact of failure and become more resilient in the face of setbacks.

Finally, seeking support and guidance from others can be a powerful tool in overcoming the fear of failure. By surrounding ourselves with people who encourage us and provide constructive feedback, we can build the confidence and resilience needed to take risks and pursue our goals.

In summary, overcoming the fear of failure is crucial to building passive income. By recognizing that failure is a natural part of the learning process, shifting our mindset, and seeking support from others, we can become more resilient and better equipped to pursue our dreams.

Overcoming the fear of failure is a common struggle for many people, and it can be difficult to know where to start. Here are some things that many people may not know about overcoming the fear of failure:

Failure is a normal part of the learning process: It's important to remember that failure is not the end of the road, but rather a part of the process. Every successful person has failed at some point, and learning from those failures is what has allowed them to ultimately succeed.

Focus on progress, not perfection: Many people are afraid of failure because they fear they won't be perfect. Instead of striving for perfection, focus on making progress towards your goals. Celebrate small successes and use them as motivation to keep moving forward.

Embrace your mistakes: When you make a mistake, it can be tempting to beat yourself up over it. However, it's important to remember that mistakes are opportunities for growth and learning. Embrace your mistakes and use them as a chance to improve.

Take action: One of the best ways to overcome the fear of failure is to take action. Often, we fear failure because we're unsure of what will happen if we try. Taking action can help to dispel some of those fears and build confidence in ourselves.

Surround yourself with supportive people: It's important to surround yourself with people who believe in you and your goals. Having a supportive network of friends, family, or colleagues can help you to overcome your fear of failure and stay motivated to pursue your goals.

Practice self-compassion: Remember to be kind to yourself. It's okay to make mistakes and experience failure along the way. Treat yourself with the same compassion and understanding that you would offer a friend who is going through a similar experience.

Overall, overcoming the fear of failure is a journey, and it takes time and practice. By focusing on progress, embracing mistakes, taking action, surrounding yourself with supportive people, and practicing self-compassion, you can build the resilience and confidence you need to pursue your goals and achieve success.

Dealing with setbacks and obstacles

Dealing with setbacks and obstacles is an inevitable part of any journey towards success, including building passive income streams. While setbacks and obstacles can be frustrating and discouraging, they are also opportunities for growth and learning. Here are some things that many people may not know about dealing with setbacks and obstacles:

It's important to have a growth mindset: People with a growth mindset view setbacks and obstacles as opportunities for learning and growth. They see failure as a natural part of the learning process and are more likely to bounce back from setbacks.

Anticipate and prepare for obstacles: One way to deal with setbacks is to anticipate and prepare for them in advance. This means identifying potential obstacles and developing a plan for how to overcome them.

Learn from the experience: Every setback and obstacle provides an opportunity to learn and improve. Take time to reflect on what went wrong, what could have been done differently, and what you can do better next time.

Don't give up: It can be tempting to give up when faced with setbacks and obstacles, but persistence is key. It's important to stay committed to your goals and keep working towards them, even when things get tough.

Seek support: Dealing with setbacks and obstacles can be challenging, and it's important to have a support system in place. This can be friends, family, a mentor, or a coach who can offer encouragement and guidance.

Focus on what you can control: While setbacks and obstacles may be out of your control, it's important to focus on what you can control. This means identifying the actions you can take to overcome the obstacle and focusing on those actions.

Take care of yourself: Dealing with setbacks and obstacles can be emotionally and mentally draining, so it's important to take care of yourself. This means getting enough rest, eating well, exercising, and doing things that bring you joy and relaxation.

Remember, setbacks and obstacles are a natural part of any journey towards success. By adopting a growth mindset, anticipating obstacles, learning from experience, staying persistent, seeking support, focusing on what you can control, and taking care of yourself, you can overcome any obstacle and continue on your path towards building passive income.

Dealing with setbacks and obstacles is an important skill to have when building passive income streams or pursuing any kind of goal. Here are some things that many people may not know about handling setbacks and obstacles:

Setbacks and obstacles are a normal part of the process: When you embark on any new venture, setbacks and obstacles are inevitable.

It's important to remember that these are a normal part of the process and not a sign of failure.

Reframe your thinking: Instead of viewing setbacks and obstacles as a negative thing, try to reframe your thinking and see them as an opportunity for growth and learning. Each setback can teach you something new and help you improve your approach.

Don't give up: It can be tempting to give up when faced with a setback or obstacle, but it's important to keep going. Persistence is key when building passive income streams or pursuing any goal.

Learn from others: It can be helpful to seek out advice and guidance from others who have faced similar setbacks and obstacles. There may be strategies and techniques that you can learn from their experiences.

Stay flexible: When faced with obstacles or setbacks, it's important to be flexible and willing to adjust your approach. This may involve trying new strategies or changing your goals, but it's important to stay open to new possibilities.

Take care of yourself: Dealing with setbacks and obstacles can be stressful, so it's important to take care of yourself during these times. Make sure you are getting enough rest, exercise, and nutrition to help you stay resilient and focused.

Celebrate your successes: It's important to take time to celebrate your successes, no matter how small they may be. Celebrating your progress can help you stay motivated and focused, and can also help you see the bigger picture when faced with setbacks and obstacles.

Staying motivated and consistent

Staying motivated and consistent is crucial for success in any endeavor, including building passive income streams. However, it's not always easy to stay motivated and remain consistent, especially when faced with setbacks and challenges. Here are some lesser-known tips for staying motivated and consistent when building passive income:

Focus on the big picture: It's important to keep your long-term goals in mind when you're feeling unmotivated or frustrated. Remind yourself why you started building passive income in the first place, and how it will help you achieve your bigger life goals.

Create a routine: Establishing a daily routine can help you stay consistent and make progress towards your goals. This routine can include specific times for working on your passive income projects, as well as time for self-care and relaxation.

Find an accountability partner: Having someone to hold you accountable can be a powerful motivator. Find someone who shares your goals or is also building passive income, and check in with each other regularly to share progress and offer support.

Celebrate small wins: Celebrating small successes along the way can help you stay motivated and focused on your progress. Take time to acknowledge your accomplishments, even if they seem small.

Learn from failures: Setbacks and failures are inevitable, but they can also provide valuable lessons. Rather than letting failures discourage you, use them as an opportunity to learn and improve your approach.

Practice self-compassion: It's easy to be hard on yourself when things don't go as planned, but self-compassion is key to staying motivated and consistent. Treat yourself with kindness and understanding, and remember that building passive income is a process that takes time and effort.

Seek inspiration and motivation: Surrounding yourself with inspiring people, books, podcasts, or other resources can help you stay motivated and focused on your goals. Seek out content that resonates with you and inspires you to keep going.

By applying these tips and techniques, you can overcome the challenges of building passive income and stay motivated and consistent towards achieving your goals.

Establishing a routine: Having a consistent schedule can help keep you on track and establish good habits. This can include setting aside specific times of day to work on your passive income projects, as well as scheduling breaks and time for self-care.

Tracking progress: Keeping track of your progress can help you stay motivated by showing you how far you've come and what you still need to do. This can also help you identify any areas where you may be struggling and need to make adjustments.

Celebrating small wins: Celebrating even small accomplishments can help boost your motivation and give you the confidence to keep going. This can include treating yourself to something small or simply acknowledging your progress and giving yourself a pat on the back.

Surrounding yourself with supportive people: Having a supportive network of friends and family can help keep you motivated and provide encouragement when you need it. You can also consider joining a community or support group focused on passive income strategies to connect with like-minded individuals.

Focusing on the bigger picture

When you hit roadblocks or encounter setbacks, it can be helpful to focus on your long-term goals and the reasons why you started pursuing passive income in the first place. This can help you stay motivated and maintain perspective during challenging times.

Focusing on the big picture is an important aspect of achieving success in any area of life, including building passive income streams. However, many people may not realize the full scope of what it means to focus on the big picture.

One important aspect of focusing on the big picture is setting long-term goals and creating a plan to achieve them. This involves taking a step back and considering what you want to achieve in the future, whether it's financial independence, the ability to travel or spend more time with family, or simply the freedom to pursue your passions without worrying about money. Once you have a clear understanding of your long-term goals, you can start to develop a plan for achieving them by breaking them down into smaller, more manageable steps.

Another key aspect of focusing on the big picture is staying committed to your goals over the long term. This requires developing a mindset that is focused on the future and willing to put in the work and effort required to achieve your goals. It also involves maintaining a positive attitude and staying motivated, even when faced with setbacks or obstacles along the way.

In addition to these more practical aspects of focusing on the big picture, it's also important to cultivate a sense of purpose and meaning in your life. This involves thinking about the kind of impact you want to have on the world and the legacy you want to leave behind. By aligning your goals with your personal values and beliefs, you can create a sense of meaning and purpose that will help you stay motivated and focused even during challenging times.

Overall, focusing on the big picture is about taking a holistic approach to your life and your goals, and developing the mindset and habits that will help you achieve success and fulfillment over the long term.

One important thing many people may not know about focusing on the big picture is that it requires a certain level of detachment from day-to-day distractions and stressors. It can be challenging to keep your eyes on the long-term goals when you're bogged down by the minutiae of daily life.

To counteract this, it's essential to have a clear vision of what you want to achieve and a plan for how you will get there. Break your long-term goals down into smaller, achievable steps that you can work towards every day.

Another crucial aspect of focusing on the big picture is the ability to adapt to change. The world is constantly evolving, and unforeseen circumstances can throw a wrench into even the most well-laid plans. You must be able to adjust your strategies and pivot as needed while keeping your end goal in sight.

Finally, it's important to celebrate small wins along the way. Focusing on the big picture can be daunting, but recognizing the progress you're making can help keep you motivated and energized. Remember that every step forward, no matter how small, brings you closer to your ultimate goal.

Being open to learning and trying new things: The world of passive income is constantly evolving, and it's important to stay up-to-date on new trends and opportunities. Being open to trying new things and expanding your skillset can help you stay competitive and find success in this field.

Maintaining a work-life balance

Maintaining a work-life balance is an important aspect of achieving overall happiness and success. However, many people struggle with finding the right balance, especially when working on building passive income streams or running a business.

One thing many people may not know is that a work-life balance does not always mean dividing your time equally between work and personal life. It's about finding a balance that works for you and your unique situation. This may mean putting in more work hours during certain times of the year to meet business goals, but also taking the necessary time off to recharge and take care of personal needs.

Another important aspect is setting boundaries. When building passive income streams or running a business, it can be easy to let work consume all your time and energy. However, it's important to set boundaries and stick to them. This may mean scheduling in specific times for work and personal activities, avoiding checking emails or working during designated personal time, or delegating tasks to others to free up your time.

Prioritization is also key in maintaining a work-life balance. This means understanding what's most important to you and focusing on those things. For example, if spending time with family is a top priority, then making time for family activities should be a non-negotiable part of your schedule.

Lastly, taking care of your physical and mental health is crucial in maintaining a work-life balance. This includes getting enough sleep, exercising regularly, and taking time for relaxation and self-care activities. Prioritizing these activities can help you feel more energized and motivated to tackle work and personal tasks.

Overall, maintaining a work-life balance requires intentionality and consistent effort. It may take some trial and error to find the right balance for your unique situation, but it's worth it for your overall well-being and success.

Set Boundaries: It's essential to set clear boundaries between your work and personal life. This means establishing designated work hours and sticking to them, not checking work-related emails or messages during non-work hours, and communicating with colleagues and clients about your availability.

Prioritize: It's important to prioritize your responsibilities and focus on the most critical tasks first. This way, you can ensure that you are making progress in your work while still having time for your personal life.

Delegate: Learn to delegate tasks to others, whether at work or in your personal life. Delegating can free up more time for you to focus on what matters most and can help prevent burnout.

Take Breaks: It's crucial to take regular breaks throughout the day to rest and recharge. Whether it's a short walk, a quick workout, or just some time to decompress, breaks can help you be more productive and focused.

Practice Self-Care: Make sure to take care of yourself by eating healthy, exercising, and getting enough sleep. These habits can help you maintain energy and focus throughout the day and keep you feeling your best.

Be Present: When you're spending time with family or friends, try to be fully present and engaged. This can help you maintain strong relationships and prevent burnout.

Learn to Say No: It's important to learn to say no to requests or commitments that don't align with your priorities or values. This can help you avoid overcommitting yourself and feeling overwhelmed.

Plan Ahead: Finally, it's essential to plan ahead and schedule your time to ensure you are making time for both work and personal life. This way, you can be intentional about how you spend your time and avoid feeling pulled in too many directions at once.

Building a support network

Building a support network is an essential aspect of achieving success in any field. It involves surrounding oneself with people who provide encouragement, motivation, and advice, and can help overcome challenges and setbacks. However, there are a few things that many people do not know about building a support network.

Firstly, building a support network requires a proactive approach. It is essential to seek out and cultivate relationships with people who share similar goals and values. This could involve attending networking events, joining professional organizations, or participating in online communities.

Secondly, it is important to have a diverse support network that includes individuals from different backgrounds and with different perspectives. This can provide a more comprehensive perspective on challenges and opportunities and enable one to make better-informed decisions.

Thirdly, a support network does not necessarily have to consist of people in the same industry or field. Often, people in different professions or industries can provide valuable insights and advice.

Fourthly, it is crucial to maintain relationships with one's support network continually. This means keeping in touch regularly, providing support when needed, and showing appreciation for their contributions.

Lastly, it is essential to give back to one's support network by offering support, advice, and assistance when needed. This helps to build stronger relationships and strengthens the support network for everyone involved.

In summary, building a support network requires a proactive approach, a diverse group of individuals, and the maintenance of ongoing relationships. It can provide invaluable support, motivation, and advice that can help individuals achieve success in their personal and professional lives.

Building a support network is an essential part of achieving success and reaching your goals. However, many people underestimate the importance of having a support network and may not know how to go about building one.

One thing that many people do not know is that building a support network does not necessarily mean having a large group of people around you. It is better to have a small group of people who are genuinely supportive and can help you stay on track.

Another important aspect of building a support network is finding people who have experience in the areas where you need help. For example, if you are starting a business, you may want to seek out mentors or other entrepreneurs who have been through the process before.

It is also essential to build relationships with people who share your values and goals. This can help you stay motivated and focused, and you can provide each other with encouragement and support.

Networking events and online communities are great places to meet people who can help you build a support network. Attending conferences and industry events can also be helpful for making connections and learning from others.

In addition to finding mentors and peers, it is also important to seek support from family and friends. Having a strong support network at home can help you deal with stress and maintain a positive outlook.

Finally, it is important to remember that building a support network is a two-way street. You should also be willing to support and help others in your network when they need it. Building a strong support network is not just about receiving help, but also about giving back and building mutually beneficial relationships.

PART 7
Tips and Tricks for Maximizing Your Passive Income Potential

CHAPTER *8*

TIPS AND TRICKS FOR MAXIMIZING YOUR PASSIVE INCOME POTENTIAL

When it comes to maximizing your passive income potential, there are several tips and tricks that you can use to increase your earnings. Here are a few things that many people may not know:

Diversify your income streams

Don't put all your eggs in one basket. Try to diversify your passive income streams by investing in different types of assets, such as stocks, real estate, and businesses.

Diversifying your passive income streams is a common piece of advice, but what many people may not know is that diversification should not only occur across different asset classes but also within them. For example, if you invest in the stock market, it is not enough to simply buy stocks from different companies. You should also consider investing in different sectors, such as healthcare, technology, and energy, to reduce the risk of losing money in case of a market downturn in one particular sector.

Similarly, when it comes to real estate investing, diversification can mean investing in different types of properties, such as residential, commercial, and industrial properties, in different locations, and with different types of tenants. This helps to spread out your risk and protect your income in case of a downturn in one particular real estate market.

It is also important to consider diversifying the types of passive income streams you have. Don't rely solely on one type of income, such as rental income from properties, but also consider other options like affiliate marketing, selling digital products, or investing in dividend-paying stocks. This helps to spread out your income sources and reduce your overall risk.

Overall, diversifying your passive income streams can help you achieve a more stable and resilient income portfolio, reducing your exposure to risk and maximizing your potential for long-term financial success.

Identify your risk tolerance: Before investing in any new asset, make sure to evaluate your risk tolerance. Different types of investments come with varying degrees of risk, so it's important to understand how much risk you are willing to take on.

Consider your expertise: When diversifying your income streams, consider investing in assets that align with your expertise. For example, if you have experience in real estate, consider investing in rental properties or REITs (real estate investment trusts).

Do your research: Don't jump into any investment without doing your due diligence first. Research the market, the asset, and any potential risks associated with the investment.

Start small: It's always a good idea to start small when investing in a new asset. This allows you to learn the ropes and minimize any potential losses.

Keep track of your investments: Make sure to regularly review your investment portfolio and track your progress. This can help you identify any underperforming assets and make necessary adjustments to your strategy.

Overall, diversifying your income streams can help you minimize risk and maximize your potential for passive income. By investing in a variety of assets, you can create a more stable and resilient financial future.

Automate your income

Use tools and systems to automate your passive income streams, such as using a platform like Patreon to manage your recurring income from fans or using an online course platform to sell your courses.

One thing many people may not know about automating their income is that it's not a one-and-done process. While there are tools and systems available to automate passive income streams, it's important to regularly monitor and adjust these systems to ensure they're working effectively.

For example, if you're using a platform like Patreon to manage your recurring income, it's important to regularly update your content and engage with your supporters to keep them interested and motivated to continue supporting you. Similarly, if you're selling courses on an online platform, it's important to regularly update and promote your courses to ensure a steady flow of sales.

Additionally, it's important to not rely solely on automation and to still put effort into your passive income streams. While automation can save time and effort, it's not a substitute for creating high-quality content or products that will attract and retain customers. Regularly updating and improving your content or products is crucial for maintaining and growing your passive income streams over time.

Consider outsourcing: In addition to using tools and systems to automate your income, you can also consider outsourcing some tasks to free up your time and focus on generating more income. For example, you can hire a virtual assistant to handle administrative tasks or a content creator to produce content for your website or social media channels.

Use technology to your advantage: There are numerous apps and tools that can help you automate your income streams. For example, you can use an app like IFTTT (If This Then That) to automate certain tasks, like sending out automated emails or posting to social media.

Monitor and adjust: While automating your income streams can save you time and effort, it's important to monitor them regularly to ensure they are performing as expected. If you notice any issues or opportunities for improvement, adjust your strategy accordingly.

Keep learning: As technology continues to evolve, there are always new tools and strategies emerging to help you automate your income streams more effectively. Make it a priority to stay up-to-date on the latest trends and techniques so you can continually improve your passive income generation.

Continuously educate yourself: Keep learning and educating yourself on new and innovative ways to create passive income streams. Attend seminars, read books and blogs, and watch online courses to stay updated.

Leverage the power of the internet: Take advantage of the internet to reach a wider audience and market your products or services. You can use social media, search engine optimization, and email marketing to increase your reach.

Network with like-minded individuals: Join groups and communities of like-minded people who are interested in creating passive income. You can learn from them and also find potential partners for future projects.

Be patient and persistent: Passive income is not a get-rich-quick scheme. It takes time and effort to build a sustainable passive income stream. Don't give up too quickly, and keep pushing forward even when things get tough.

Outsource tasks: If you find yourself overwhelmed with tasks, consider outsourcing some of the work to others. This can free up your time to focus on other income-generating activities.

Keep track of your finances

Stay organized and keep track of your expenses and income to ensure that you are making a profit from your passive income streams. Use tools like accounting software or hire a professional accountant if necessary.

One thing that many people may not know is the importance of keeping detailed records of their passive income streams. While it can be tempting to let these income streams operate on autopilot, it's important to monitor them closely to ensure they are profitable and sustainable over time.

In addition to using accounting software or hiring a professional accountant, there are other tools and strategies that can help with tracking finances. For example, setting up separate bank accounts or credit cards for each passive income stream can help keep things organized and make it easier to track expenses and income.

Another tip is to regularly review and analyze financial data to identify areas for improvement and opportunities for growth. This can involve setting financial goals for each income stream, tracking progress over time, and adjusting strategies as needed to maximize profitability.

Overall, the key is to be proactive and diligent in managing finances for passive income streams, even when they seem to be running smoothly on their own. By doing so, individuals can ensure they are maximizing their income potential and building a solid foundation for long-term financial stability.

Separate your personal and business finances: It's important to have separate bank accounts and credit cards for your personal and business finances. This makes it easier to track your business expenses and income, and helps you avoid mixing personal expenses with business expenses.

Use accounting software: Accounting software can help you track your expenses, income, and profits, and generate financial reports. Some popular options include QuickBooks, Xero, and FreshBooks.

Hire a professional accountant: If you're not comfortable managing your own finances or have a complex financial situation, consider hiring a professional accountant. They can help you with tasks such as bookkeeping, tax preparation, and financial planning.

Keep receipts and records: It's important to keep records of all your business expenses and income, including receipts, invoices, and bank statements. This makes it easier to track your finances and provides documentation in case of an audit.

Monitor your cash flow: Cash flow is the movement of money in and out of your business. It's important to monitor your cash flow regularly to ensure that you have enough money to cover expenses and invest in your business.

Create a budget: A budget can help you plan your expenses and income, and ensure that you're not overspending. Make sure to include all your expenses, such as rent, utilities, and marketing costs, and factor in your expected income.

Review your finances regularly: Make sure to review your finances regularly, such as monthly or quarterly, to track your progress and identify areas for improvement. This can help you make better decisions about your passive income streams and ensure that you're meeting your financial goals.

Set up automatic payments: If you have recurring expenses, such as website hosting fees or software subscriptions, consider setting up automatic payments to ensure that you never miss a payment. This can also help you stay on top of your finances and avoid any late fees.

Regularly review your finances: Make it a habit to regularly review your finances and assess the performance of your passive income streams. This can help you identify any areas for improvement and make any necessary adjustments to maximize your earnings.

Test and optimize your strategies: Continuously test and optimize your passive income strategies to find the ones that work best for you. Keep track of your results and adjust your approach as needed to maximize your earnings.

By following these tips and tricks, you can increase your chances of success in building and maximizing your passive income potential.

Using automation tools and software

Automation tools and software have become increasingly popular in recent years, as they can help businesses and individuals save time and increase efficiency. There are various types of automation tools and software available for different tasks, such as marketing automation, social media automation, email automation, and task automation.

One of the benefits of using automation tools and software is that they can help you streamline repetitive tasks and processes, freeing up time for more important tasks. For example, marketing automation software can automate email campaigns, lead generation, and lead nurturing, while social media automation tools can help you schedule and publish posts across multiple social media platforms.

Another benefit of using automation tools and software is that they can help you improve your data analysis and decision-making processes. For example, data analysis tools can help you analyze large amounts of data quickly and efficiently, allowing you to identify trends and make informed decisions based on real-time data.

However, it's important to note that automation tools and software should be used strategically and carefully. While they can be helpful, they should not be relied on completely and should be monitored regularly to ensure that they are working properly and not causing any issues.

Additionally, it's important to choose the right automation tools and software for your specific needs and goals. Not all tools and software are created equal, and some may be better suited for certain tasks than others. It's important to do your research and carefully evaluate different options before making a decision.

Overall, automation tools and software can be incredibly helpful for streamlining tasks, increasing efficiency, and improving decision-making processes. However, they should be used strategically and carefully to ensure that they are benefiting your business or personal goals.

Automation tools and software are becoming increasingly popular in various industries as they allow for repetitive and time-consuming tasks to be completed quickly and efficiently. In terms of passive income, automation can help streamline processes and increase productivity, resulting in more income-generating opportunities.

One way to use automation tools is to automate marketing efforts. For example, social media scheduling tools like Hootsuite or Buffer can help schedule posts ahead of time, ensuring consistent and regular content creation without the need for constant manual effort. Email marketing tools like Mailchimp or Constant Contact can also automate the process of sending out newsletters and promotional emails to subscribers.

Another way to use automation tools is to automate financial management. Many banks and financial institutions offer automatic savings plans that can transfer a portion of income directly into a savings account or investment account. Budgeting apps like Mint or YNAB can also help automate the process of tracking expenses and managing finances.

Additionally, there are automation tools available for specific passive income streams such as affiliate marketing. For example, affiliate networks like Commission Junction or ShareASale offer tools that automate the process of tracking clicks, sales, and commissions.

Overall, automation tools and software can help save time and increase efficiency, ultimately leading to more opportunities for passive income generation. However, it is important to use these tools responsibly and monitor their effectiveness regularly to ensure that they are contributing to overall profitability.

Diversifying your passive income streams

Diversifying your passive income streams is an essential strategy to minimize risk and maximize returns. However, many people may not realize that diversification goes beyond investing in different types of assets. It also means having multiple streams of passive income from various sources.

One way to diversify your passive income streams is by investing in different types of assets, such as stocks, bonds, real estate, and businesses. Each asset class has its own risk and return profile, so by spreading your investments across multiple asset classes, you can minimize the impact of any one asset class's performance on your overall portfolio.

Another way to diversify your passive income streams is by investing in different types of real estate properties. You can invest in commercial real estate, residential real estate, or even vacation rentals. Each type of property has its own unique advantages and disadvantages, so by investing in a mix of properties, you can create a well-rounded portfolio that can withstand market fluctuations.

Furthermore, you can also diversify your passive income streams by investing in different types of businesses, such as franchises, startups, or existing businesses. Each business has its own risk and return profile, so by investing in a mix of businesses, you can reduce the impact of any one business's performance on your overall income.

In addition to diversifying your assets and income streams, you can also diversify your passive income by exploring different passive income models, such as affiliate marketing, dropshipping, digital product sales, or licensing your intellectual property.

Overall, diversification is key to creating a stable and sustainable passive income portfolio. By investing in a mix of assets, businesses, and passive income models, you can minimize risk and maximize returns over the long run.

Consider investing in alternative assets: While stocks and real estate are popular passive income streams, there are many other options out there that can help diversify your portfolio. These include things like peer-to-peer lending, cryptocurrency, and even investing in fine art or collectibles.

Look for passive income opportunities within your existing assets: If you already own a rental property, for example, you could look for ways to increase your passive income from that asset. This could include adding additional units or amenities, raising rent, or exploring short-term rentals.

Think outside the box: There are many creative ways to generate passive income that don't involve traditional investments or assets. For example, you could create a course or ebook on a topic you're knowledgeable about and sell it online, or start a YouTube channel and earn ad revenue.

Don't forget about recurring income: Many passive income streams are one-time payouts, but recurring income can be a powerful way to build long-term wealth. This might include things like affiliate marketing or earning royalties from intellectual property.

Be mindful of your risk tolerance: Diversification is important, but it's also important to consider your risk tolerance. Investing in high-risk assets may offer the potential for high returns, but it also comes with a greater chance of loss. Make sure you're comfortable with the level of risk involved in each passive income stream you pursue.

Staying up-to-date on industry trends and changes

Staying up-to-date on industry trends and changes is crucial for anyone looking to build and maintain passive income streams. Here are some things many people may not know about this topic:

Industry trends and changes can have a significant impact on your passive income streams: For example, changes in search engine algorithms can affect your website's traffic, and new regulations can impact your real estate investments.

Keeping up-to-date with industry trends can help you spot new opportunities for passive income: For example, if you notice that people are increasingly interested in sustainable products, you might decide to start a business selling eco-friendly items.

There are many ways to stay up-to-date on industry trends: You can attend industry conferences and events, subscribe to trade publications and newsletters, and follow thought leaders and experts in your field on social media.

You should also pay attention to consumer trends: Knowing what your target audience wants and needs can help you create passive income streams that are in demand and likely to be successful.

Staying up-to-date on industry trends and changes requires ongoing effort: Trends and changes can happen quickly, so it's important to regularly check in on what's happening in your industry and adjust your strategies as needed.

Finally, staying up-to-date on industry trends can help you future-proof your passive income streams: By being aware of upcoming changes, you can prepare your business or investments to withstand and even thrive in the face of challenges or disruptions.

Staying up-to-date on industry trends and changes is crucial for anyone looking to build and maintain passive income streams. Here are some things that many people may not know about staying informed:

Utilize multiple sources: To stay informed on industry trends and changes, it's important to gather information from multiple sources. This can include industry publications, blogs, social media, and professional networks. By utilizing a variety of sources, you can get a more comprehensive understanding of what's happening in your industry.

Attend conferences and events: Attending conferences and events in your industry is a great way to stay up-to-date on the latest trends and changes. These events often feature industry experts and thought leaders who can provide valuable insights and perspectives. Additionally, networking at these events can lead to new opportunities and connections.

Join professional organizations: Joining professional organizations in your industry can also provide valuable insights and networking opportunities. Many organizations offer newsletters, webinars, and other resources that can help you stay informed on industry trends and changes.

Follow thought leaders and influencers: Following thought leaders and influencers in your industry can be a great way to stay informed on the latest trends and changes. These individuals often share their insights and perspectives on social media, blogs, and other platforms.

Stay informed on new technologies: Many industries are rapidly evolving due to advances in technology. It's important to stay informed on new technologies and how they are affecting your industry. This can include attending technology-focused events, following industry blogs and publications that cover technology, and participating in online forums and discussions.

By staying informed on industry trends and changes, you can identify new opportunities for passive income streams and ensure that your existing streams remain relevant and profitable.

Building strong relationships with customers and clients

Building strong relationships with customers and clients is essential for any business, whether it is a traditional or passive income stream. Many people may not realize that building relationships with customers and clients can actually be a part of their passive income strategy.

One way to build relationships with customers and clients is through email marketing. By creating an email list and sending out regular newsletters, businesses can keep their customers and clients updated on new products or services, promotions, and other news. This can help to build trust and loyalty among customers and keep them coming back for more.

Another way to build strong relationships is through social media. By engaging with customers and clients on social media platforms such as Facebook, Twitter, and Instagram, businesses can establish a personal connection with their audience. This can lead to increased brand awareness, customer loyalty, and ultimately, increased revenue.

Additionally, businesses can offer excellent customer service to build strong relationships with customers and clients. Responding quickly and effectively to customer inquiries, complaints, and feedback can help to establish trust and show that the business values its customers. This can also lead to positive word-of-mouth referrals and increased business.

Overall, building strong relationships with customers and clients is essential for any passive income strategy. By focusing on building trust and loyalty, businesses can increase customer retention, which can lead to increased revenue and a more successful passive income stream.

In addition to the tips mentioned earlier, there are a few more things to keep in mind when it comes to building strong relationships with customers and clients:

Communicate clearly and effectively: Make sure you are communicating with your customers and clients in a way that is clear and easy to understand. Use language that is appropriate for your audience, and always be responsive to their questions and concerns.

Show appreciation: Take the time to thank your customers and clients for their business and show that you value their support. This could be as simple as sending a personalized thank-you email or offering a special discount on their next purchase.

Provide exceptional customer service: Be sure to go above and beyond to meet the needs of your customers and clients. This could mean offering additional support, providing detailed product information, or even offering free samples or trials to new customers.

Address concerns and complaints promptly: No matter how great your products or services are, there will inevitably be times when customers or clients have concerns or complaints. When this happens, it's important to address these issues promptly and professionally to show that you care about their satisfaction.

Build a community: Consider creating a community around your brand or products. This could involve creating a Facebook group, hosting webinars or live events, or even partnering with influencers or other businesses in your industry to build a larger network of supporters and customers.

Investing in education and self-improvement

Investing in education and self-improvement is a crucial step towards building a successful career and achieving financial freedom. However, many people overlook the importance of this step and underestimate its value in building passive income streams. Here are some things that many people may not know about investing in education and self-improvement:

Education doesn't have to be expensive: While formal education can be expensive, there are many affordable options for gaining new skills and knowledge. Online courses, books, and free resources like podcasts and blogs can be a great way to learn new things without breaking the bank.

Learning doesn't stop after graduation: Even if you have a degree, it's important to continue learning and improving your skills to stay relevant in your industry. This could mean attending conferences and workshops, taking additional courses, or pursuing certifications.

Self-improvement goes beyond education: Building passive income requires more than just knowledge and skills. It also requires a strong work ethic, time management skills, and the ability to persevere through challenges. Investing in personal development through activities like meditation, exercise, or therapy can help you develop these qualities and become a more effective entrepreneur.

Networking is a crucial part of education and self-improvement: Building relationships with others in your industry can provide valuable insights and opportunities. Attend industry events, join professional organizations, and connect with others online to expand your network and learn from others.

Overall, investing in education and self-improvement is a valuable way to build passive income streams. By continuously learning and growing, you can stay ahead of industry trends, build a strong reputation, and position yourself for success.

Investing in education and self-improvement is crucial to achieving success in any field, including passive income generation. Here are some additional things that many people may not know about investing in education and self-improvement:

It's not just about formal education: While traditional education such as attending college or university can be beneficial, investing in education and self-improvement can also involve attending seminars, reading books, taking online courses, and learning from mentors or experts in your field. There are many ways to gain knowledge and improve your skills outside of traditional education.

Learning is a lifelong process: Investing in education and self-improvement is not a one-time thing. It's important to continuously seek out new knowledge and skills to stay relevant in your industry and adapt to changing trends and technologies.

It can help you identify new opportunities: By investing in education and self-improvement, you can expand your knowledge and expertise, which can help you identify new opportunities for passive income generation. For example, by learning about the latest digital marketing strategies, you may discover new ways to promote your online business and increase your passive income streams.

It can improve your confidence: Building your knowledge and skills can improve your confidence in your abilities, which can help you take risks and pursue new opportunities for passive income generation.

It can lead to personal growth: Investing in education and self-improvement can also lead to personal growth and development. By learning new things and challenging yourself, you can gain a better understanding of yourself and your values, which can help you make better decisions in all areas of your life, including passive income generation.

PART 8
Case Studies and Success Stories

CHAPTER *9*

CASE STUDIES AND SUCCESS STORIES

Case studies and success stories are powerful tools for learning and inspiration in various fields, including business, entrepreneurship, and personal development. Many people may not fully realize the benefits and opportunities that come with studying and analyzing case studies and success stories.

Firstly, case studies offer a unique perspective into real-world situations, allowing readers to examine specific challenges, strategies, and outcomes in detail. This can provide valuable insights into different industries and business models, highlighting successful approaches and identifying potential pitfalls. Additionally, case studies can help readers develop critical thinking skills, as they must analyze information and draw conclusions based on evidence.

Success stories, on the other hand, offer inspiration and motivation for individuals looking to achieve their own goals. By reading about the experiences and journeys of successful entrepreneurs, investors, and professionals, readers can gain valuable insights into what it takes to succeed and how to overcome challenges along the way. Success stories can also provide a sense of community and connection, as readers can identify with the struggles and triumphs of those who have achieved success.

Moreover, case studies and success stories can provide a platform for networking and collaboration. By sharing their stories and experiences, successful individuals can attract potential partners, investors, and customers who are interested in their work. This can help them expand their business and achieve even greater success.

In conclusion, case studies and success stories offer a wealth of benefits for individuals looking to learn, grow, and succeed. They provide a unique and valuable perspective into real-world situations, offer inspiration and motivation, develop critical thinking skills, and can provide networking and collaboration opportunities. It's important to seek out and study these resources to gain valuable insights and achieve your own goals.

Case studies and success stories can provide valuable insights and inspiration for individuals looking to build their passive income streams. However, it is important to approach these stories with a critical eye and to understand the context and circumstances that led to their success.

Many people may not know that success stories often involve a combination of factors, including hard work, strategic planning, timing, and sometimes luck. It is important to recognize that what worked for one person may not necessarily work for another, and that there are no guarantees of success.

Moreover, it is important to consider the potential downsides and risks associated with any passive income strategy, even those that have been successful for others. For example, investing in real estate may come with the risk of property damage or liability issues, while investing in the stock market may involve market volatility and potential losses.

That being said, case studies and success stories can still provide valuable insights and inspiration, as long as they are approached with a critical eye and used as a starting point for further research and analysis. By studying successful individuals and businesses, one can gain a better understanding of the strategies and tactics that have worked for them, and potentially apply those insights to their own passive income pursuits.

Interviews with successful passive income earners

Interviews with successful passive income earners can provide valuable insights and tips for those looking to build their own passive income streams. Here are some things many people may not know about this topic:

Real-life examples: Interviews with successful passive income earners provide real-life examples of people who have successfully built passive income streams. These examples can be a source of inspiration and motivation for those looking to do the same.

Unique strategies: Every person's journey to building passive income is unique, and interviews with successful earners can reveal some of the strategies and techniques they used to achieve success. By listening to a variety of interviews, you can gain insights into the different approaches people take to building passive income.

Mistakes and lessons learned: Successful passive income earners often share their mistakes and lessons learned along the way. This can be incredibly valuable for those starting out, as they can learn from others' mistakes and avoid making the same ones.

Personal stories: Interviews with successful passive income earners often include personal stories and anecdotes that provide context and background for their journey. These stories can help listeners connect with the interviewee on a deeper level and understand the challenges they faced and overcame.

Practical advice: Along with personal stories and unique strategies, interviews with successful passive income earners often provide practical advice and tips that listeners can apply to their own lives. From advice on investing to tips for building an audience, these interviews can offer a wealth of knowledge for those looking to build their own passive income streams.

Overall, interviews with successful passive income earners offer a valuable window into the world of passive income and can provide inspiration, motivation, and practical advice for those looking to build their own streams of passive income.

One thing that many people may not know about interviews with successful passive income earners is that they can offer valuable insights and advice beyond just the technical details of their strategies. These interviews can provide a glimpse into the mindset and habits of successful entrepreneurs, which can be just as important as the tactics they use.

For example, successful passive income earners may share their daily routines, how they stay motivated, and how they approach risk-taking and failure. They may also offer tips on how to build relationships with customers and clients, manage time effectively, and balance work and life responsibilities.

In addition, interviews with successful passive income earners can provide inspiration and motivation for those looking to start their own passive income journey. Hearing about the successes and challenges of others who have achieved financial freedom can help to build confidence and give people the push they need to take action towards their own goals.

Overall, interviews with successful passive income earners can be a valuable resource for anyone looking to learn more about building passive income streams and achieving financial independence.

Real-life examples of how people have built passive income streams from scratch

Real-life examples of how people have built passive income streams from scratch can provide valuable insights into the strategies and tactics used by successful passive income earners. While many people may be familiar with the concept of passive income, they may not know the specific steps and processes involved in creating these streams.

One thing many people may not know is that building passive income streams from scratch often requires a significant amount of effort and dedication. It's not as simple as investing in a stock or rental property and then sitting back and watching the money roll in. In most cases, building a passive income stream requires an initial investment of time and money, as well as ongoing effort to maintain and grow the stream.

Real-life examples can also help to highlight the importance of finding a niche or area of expertise to focus on. Many successful passive income earners have found success by identifying a specific need or demand in their industry and developing products or services to meet that need.

Another aspect that many people may not know is that building passive income streams often involves taking risks and trying new things. Not every strategy or investment will be successful, and it's important to be willing to learn from failures and adapt as needed.

Finally, real-life examples can demonstrate the power of persistence and determination in building passive income streams. Many successful earners did not achieve their success overnight, and often faced setbacks and obstacles along the way. However, by staying focused on their goals and continuing to put in the work, they were able to build sustainable and profitable streams of passive income.

Here are some additional insights on real-life examples of building passive income streams from scratch:

Start small and scale up: Many successful passive income earners started with a small idea or project and gradually scaled it up. For example, some started by creating a blog or YouTube channel, and then expanded into creating digital products, courses, and membership sites.

Find a niche and specialize: Successful passive income earners often focus on a specific niche or area of expertise, which helps them stand out and attract a loyal audience. For example, some focus on personal finance, while others specialize in travel or health and wellness.

Experiment and pivot: Building passive income streams requires trial and error. Successful earners often experiment with different ideas and strategies, and are not afraid to pivot if something is not working. For example, they may switch to a different business model, or focus on a different audience.

Consistency and persistence: Building passive income streams takes time and effort. Successful earners are consistent in their efforts, and persist even when things get tough. They understand that success doesn't happen overnight, and are willing to put in the work over the long term.

Embrace new technologies and platforms: As technology continues to evolve, successful passive income earners are constantly adapting and embracing new platforms and tools. For example, they may use social media to promote their products or courses, or leverage artificial intelligence and automation to streamline their business processes.

Focus on providing value: Successful passive income earners focus on providing value to their audience or customers. They understand that building a loyal following requires providing high-quality content or products that meet the needs of their target audience.

Build a team: As passive income streams grow, successful earners often build a team to help manage their business. This may include virtual assistants, content creators, or customer support staff. Building a team allows them to scale their business and focus on their areas of expertise.

Stay open to learning: Finally, successful passive income earners are always open to learning and improving their skills. They invest in education and seek out mentors and peers who can offer guidance and support along the way. They understand that there is always room for growth and improvement, and are willing to put in the effort to continue to build and scale their passive income streams.

Tips and advice from experts in the passive income field

When it comes to learning about building passive income, it's always a good idea to seek out advice and tips from experts in the field. Here are a few things that many people may not know about seeking advice from experts:

Look for experts who have experience in the specific area of passive income you are interested in. For example, if you are interested in building passive income through real estate investing, seek out experts in that field rather than experts in online business or stocks.

Don't be afraid to reach out to experts and ask for advice. Many experts are willing to help out and offer advice, especially if you are respectful and appreciative of their time.

Consider joining online communities or forums where experts and other passive income earners share tips and advice. This can be a great way to learn from a variety of sources and get different perspectives.

Be discerning when it comes to the advice you receive. Not all advice is created equal, and not all experts are equally knowledgeable. Make sure to do your own research and weigh the advice you receive against other sources of information.

Remember that even experts have different opinions and approaches. Just because one expert recommends a certain strategy doesn't mean it will necessarily work for you. Use your own judgment and intuition when deciding which strategies to pursue.

The importance of finding the right mentor: One of the keys to success in building passive income streams is finding the right mentor who has already achieved success in the field. A mentor can provide valuable guidance, share their experiences and help avoid common mistakes.

Keep learning and evolving: The passive income field is constantly evolving, and it's important to keep learning and staying up-to-date with the latest trends, tools and techniques. Attend conferences, read books, listen to podcasts and stay connected with other professionals in the industry.

Start small and be patient: Building passive income streams takes time, effort and patience. It's important to start small, test your ideas and be willing to pivot and adapt as needed. Don't expect overnight success and be prepared to put in the work to achieve your goals.

Build a brand and reputation: Building a strong brand and reputation is essential for long-term success in the passive income field. Focus on providing value, building trust and delivering high-quality products or services.

Leverage technology and automation: Technology and automation tools can be incredibly helpful in building and managing passive income streams. Consider using tools like email marketing software, social media management platforms, and project management tools to streamline your processes and improve efficiency.

Build a team: Building a team can help you scale your passive income streams and achieve greater success. Hire freelancers or outsource tasks to trusted professionals who can help you with tasks like content creation, marketing, and customer support.

Stay focused on your goals: Finally, it's important to stay focused on your goals and avoid distractions. Stay committed to your vision and prioritize your time and resources accordingly to achieve success in the passive income field.

PART 9
Conclusion

CHAPTER *10*
RECAP OF THE IMPORTANCE OF PASSIVE INCOME

Passive income is important for several reasons, and it is crucial to understand its significance for financial stability and long-term wealth building. Here are some points to consider:

Diversification: Passive income allows you to diversify your income streams, reducing your reliance on a single source of income. This can help protect you against financial shocks such as job loss or market downturns.

Financial freedom: Passive income can provide you with the financial freedom to pursue your goals and dreams, without being tied to a traditional 9-to-5 job. It can also help you retire earlier or work less hours.

Long-term wealth building: Passive income streams can help you build wealth over time, without the need for constant effort and active involvement.

Opportunity for growth: Passive income streams can provide opportunities for growth and expansion, allowing you to increase your income over time.

Better work-life balance: Passive income streams can provide you with the flexibility to work from anywhere and at any time, enabling you to have a better work-life balance.

It's important to remember that building passive income streams takes time and effort, and there is no single path to success.

However, by learning from experts, staying up-to-date on industry trends, diversifying your income streams, and investing in education and self-improvement, you can create a sustainable and profitable passive income portfolio that supports your financial goals and dreams.

Final thoughts and encouragement for readers to take action

Final thoughts and encouragement for readers to take action are crucial components of any content related to passive income. It's one thing to provide tips and advice on how to build passive income streams, but it's another thing entirely to motivate readers to take action and start implementing those strategies.

Many people may not know that taking action is the most important step in building passive income. Reading about it, learning new strategies, and gaining knowledge are all great, but they won't result in any passive income unless action is taken.

It's also important to encourage readers to not give up too quickly. Building passive income takes time, effort, and patience. It's not something that happens overnight, and there will likely be setbacks and challenges along the way. However, with persistence and a willingness to learn and adapt, anyone can build a successful passive income stream.

Lastly, it's important to remind readers that building passive income isn't just about making money. It's about creating a lifestyle where you have the freedom and flexibility to do what you want, when you want. It's about creating financial security and stability for yourself and your family. So, take action, be persistent, and enjoy the journey of building your passive income streams.

Start small: It can be overwhelming to think about building multiple passive income streams all at once. Start with one idea and see it through to completion before moving on to the next. Once you see progress and success, you will be motivated to continue.

Take calculated risks: Building passive income streams requires taking risks, but they should be calculated risks. Don't invest all of your money into a single venture, but don't be afraid to invest a reasonable amount to get started. If you're unsure, seek the advice of a financial professional.

Be patient: Building passive income streams takes time, effort, and patience. Don't expect overnight success, but instead focus on consistently making progress towards your goals.

Learn from failures: Not every passive income idea will be successful. Use failures as a learning opportunity to improve and make better decisions in the future.

Take action: The most important thing is to take action. Reading about passive income and learning from experts is great, but it won't get you anywhere if you don't take action. Set achievable goals and take the necessary steps to make them happen.

Remember, building passive income streams is a journey, not a destination. With persistence and dedication, anyone can achieve financial freedom and create the life they desire.

Resources and tools for building passive income

When it comes to building passive income, there are a variety of resources and tools available that many people may not know of. Here are some examples:

Online courses and tutorials: There are many online courses and tutorials available that can help individuals learn about different passive income strategies and how to implement them. These resources can be found on platforms like Udemy, Skillshare, and Coursera.

E-books and audiobooks: E-books and audiobooks can be a great resource for learning about passive income strategies and getting inspiration from successful passive income earners. Platforms like Amazon Kindle and Audible offer a wide variety of books on passive income.

Podcasts: There are many podcasts that focus on passive income strategies and feature interviews with successful passive income earners. Some popular ones include Smart Passive Income, The Side Hustle Show, and The Tim Ferriss Show.

Passive income calculators: There are several online calculators available that can help individuals estimate how much passive income they could potentially earn based on different investment strategies and scenarios.

Investment platforms: Platforms like Robinhood, Betterment, and Acorns offer easy and accessible ways to invest in stocks, mutual funds, and other assets that can generate passive income.

Networking groups and communities: Joining networking groups and online communities can provide individuals with support and guidance as they navigate their passive income journey. Platforms like Reddit and Facebook have many groups focused on passive income strategies.

Professional services: Working with professionals like financial advisors, accountants, and lawyers can help individuals make informed decisions about their passive income investments and ensure that they are complying with legal and tax regulations.

By utilizing these resources and tools, individuals can gain the knowledge and support they need to successfully build and grow their passive income streams.

Online courses and tutorials: There are many online courses and tutorials available on various platforms that teach individuals how to build and grow passive income streams. Some examples of popular platforms include Udemy, Skillshare, and Coursera.

Books: There are countless books on the topic of passive income that can provide valuable insights and strategies. Some popular titles include "The 4-Hour Work Week" by Tim Ferriss and "Rich Dad Poor Dad" by Robert Kiyosaki.

Investment platforms: There are various investment platforms available that allow individuals to invest in assets like stocks, real estate, and businesses. Some popular investment platforms include Robinhood, Fundrise, and AngelList.

Accounting software: As mentioned earlier, it's important to stay organized and keep track of your finances when building passive income streams. Accounting software like QuickBooks and Xero can help you manage your income and expenses.

Automation tools: There are numerous automation tools available that can help you streamline your passive income streams. For example, tools like Zapier and IFTTT allow you to automate tasks and workflows, while platforms like Patreon and Teachable automate aspects of selling digital products.

Networking events and conferences: Attending networking events and conferences related to your industry or niche can provide valuable opportunities to learn from experts, connect with like-minded individuals, and potentially find new business opportunities.

These are just a few examples of the resources and tools available for building passive income streams. It's important to do your research and find the resources that work best for you and your goals.

www.ingramcontent.com/pod-product-compliance
Lightning Source LLC
Chambersburg PA
CBHW031532210526
45464CB00015B/555